VACCINATION INVESTIGATION

THE HISTORY AND SCIENCE OF VACCINES

TARA HAELLE

Twenty-First Century Books / Minneapolis

FOR ALL MY FORMER STUDENTS, WHO TAUGHT
ME AS MUCH AS I HOPE I TAUGHT THEM

Twenty-First Century Books
A division of Lerner Publishing Group, Inc.
241 First Avenue North
Minneapolis, MN 55401 USA

For reading levels and more information, look up this title at www.lernerbooks.com.

Main body text set in Adobe Garamond Pro 11/15.
Typeface provided by Adobe Systems.

Library of Congress Cataloging-in-Publication Data

Library of Congress Cataloging-in-Publication Data
Names: Haelle, Tara.
Title: Vaccination investigation : the history and science of vaccines / by Tara Haelle.
Description: Minneapolis : Twenty-First Century Books, [2018] | Audience: Age 13–18. | Audience: Grade 9 to 12. | Includes bibliographical references and index.
Identifiers: LCCN 2017005193 (print) | LCCN 2017007184 (ebook) | ISBN 9781512425307 (lb : alk. paper) | ISBN 9781512498820 (eb pdf)
Subjects: LCSH: Vaccines—History—Juvenile literature. | Vaccination—History—Juvenile literature.
Classification: LCC QR189 .H34 2018 (print) | LCC QR189 (ebook) | DDC 615.3/72–dc23

LC record available at https://lccn.loc.gov/2017005193

Manufactured in the United States of America
1-41284-23243-10/2/2017

TABLE OF CONTENTS

01
VACCINE BASICS   4

02
VACCINE HISTORY   27

03
CREATING A VACCINE   44

04
PUSHBACK AGAINST VACCINES   64

05
WHAT THE FUTURE MIGHT HOLD   89

SOURCE NOTES   108

GLOSSARY   110

SELECTED BIBLIOGRAPHY   113

FURTHER INFORMATION   114

INDEX   117

01
VACCINE BASICS

James Cherry remembers what would happen, when he was a young doctor in the 1950s, when the hospital's power failed. Everyone would rush to the iron lungs, large metal chambers that pumped air in and out of the lungs of the patients lying inside. The iron lung patients could no longer breathe on their own because a disease called poliomyelitis, commonly called polio, had paralyzed their chest muscles. "They [iron lungs] had bellows that decreased the pressure in the body below the head to bring the air into their lungs," Cherry said. "If [the power] stopped, you had to do it [pump the bellows] by hand or

In the early 1950s, many US hospitals set up polio wards equipped with iron lungs. The machines pumped air in and out of the lungs of patients whose chest muscles had been paralyzed by polio.

the patient would die." It took two staffers working together to operate the bellows by hand so that the patient kept breathing.

Polio is an example of an infectious disease. Infectious diseases are those that occur when a harmful virus, bacteria, or parasite enters the body and reproduces itself. Cherry, who later became a professor at the University of California–Los Angeles School of Medicine, knew the suffering caused by infectious disease personally. His daughter was born deaf because her mother (Cherry's wife) had been infected with the rubella virus during her pregnancy. Babies born with rubella not only might be deaf but also might have intellectual disabilities. As a young doctor, Cherry went to work daily to face the ravages of meningitis, measles, and pneumonia, which were common diseases throughout the United States in the mid-twentieth century.

HOW CONTAGIOUS IS A DISEASE?

A disease that one person can get from contact with another is called a contagious disease. Some diseases are more contagious than others. Epidemiologists are scientists who study disease behavior—what can cause or prevent a disease, where it occurs, how often it occurs, how it spreads, and whom it affects. These scientists use a "basic reproduction number," abbreviated as R0, to describe how contagious a disease is. The R0 for each disease refers to how many unprotected individuals a single infected person could potentially infect. The R0 depends on how long a person with the disease is contagious. This varies by disease. The pathogen's transmission (how it travels), such as by air or through water droplets or sexual contact, also impacts the R0.

Measles is by far the most contagious human disease. The measles virus remains in the air up to two hours after an infected person leaves an area. Of those exposed to the virus in that area within that time frame, 90 percent will develop an infection. The R0 of measles is 12 to 18, which means a single person with measles typically infects 12 to 18 others who don't have immunity. Pertussis is also very contagious, with R0 estimates of 6 to 12. Diphtheria, mumps, polio, rubella, and smallpox have R0s between 5 and 7. Although Ebola is a very deadly disease, its R0 is quite low because transmission requires close contact with infected body fluids, such as blood or vomit, and a lot of people with Ebola die before there is time to transmit it to many others. Each infection therefore generates only one or two additional infections.

Some infectious diseases travel from person to person. For instance, an infected person might pass on a disease to a healthy person by sneezing, touch, or sexual contact. Other infectious diseases are transmitted by insect bites. Others come from the environment. The disease tetanus, caused by the bacteria *Clostridium tetani*, for example, lives naturally in the soil and can enter the body through a cut on the skin. Examples of other infectious diseases include chickenpox (also called varicella), the common cold, malaria, strep throat, and Zika virus. The human body's immune system—a network of cells, tissues, and organs—is designed to fight these diseases. But sometimes the diseases win the fight, leading to serious disability or even death.

Before the twentieth century, infectious disease was the number one killer of children in the United States. It was common then to have large families. Parents often had eight or more children, but due to infectious diseases, many of these children never reached adulthood. Young people who survived one infectious disease were likely to soon encounter another. By the age of twenty, they might experience a half dozen or more of the following infectious diseases: measles, polio, rubella, chickenpox, influenza, mumps, typhoid, scarlet fever, cholera, dysentery, pertussis (commonly called whooping cough for the sound infected people made when they coughed), yellow fever, malaria, diphtheria, rotavirus (the most common cause of severe diarrhea in children worldwide), pneumonia, and meningitis. For example, US president George Washington survived diphtheria at the age of fifteen, malaria at seventeen, and smallpox at nineteen. Presidents Abraham Lincoln, Grover Cleveland, and James Garfield all lost at least one child to diphtheria. In 1900 diphtheria was the tenth-leading cause of death in the United States. In that same era, about 25 percent of US children died before the age of five.

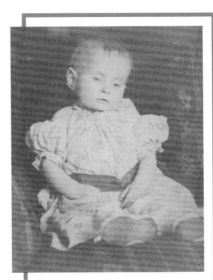

Before widespread vaccination and other public health measures, infectious diseases killed many infants. In the late nineteenth century, many families photographed their dead children to memorialize them. This child died around 1890.

Why were children the most common victims of infectious diseases? The answer involves the body's immune system. When a disease strikes someone for the first time, usually in childhood, his or her immune system is unfamiliar with it. The disease might overwhelm the immune system, leading to the child's death. Or the immune system might prevail, ridding the body of the disease. If it does, the immune system retains "memory cells" that know how to defeat the germ in the future. The child then has immunity to the disease. If it enters the body again—say after the child has grown up—the memory cells kick in and defeat the disease before symptoms even develop.

In earlier eras, the only adults who got one of the infectious diseases were those who hadn't been exposed to it as children, survived the misery, and developed immunity. Some who survived developed their immunity at a price, however. They lived with lifelong deafness, blindness, brain damage, paralysis, loss of limbs, or other disabilities from these diseases. US president Franklin D. Roosevelt (1882–1945), for example, contracted polio at the age of thirty-nine. The disease paralyzed his muscles below the waist. For the rest of his life, he relied on a wheelchair or crutches for mobility.

KNOCKING OUT INFECTIOUS DISEASES

Some infectious diseases, such as typhoid, dysentery, and cholera, are spread through germ-filled water and food. In the late nineteenth and early twentieth centuries, US cities began building sewage and indoor plumbing systems to handle waste and to pipe clean running water into and out of homes. Because families had easy access to this clean water, waterborne diseases started to disappear from the United States. US food safety laws led to cleaner, safer produce, meat, and other store-bought foods. These regulations also helped to curtail the spread of disease. Around the same time, US public health officials launched widespread programs to spray insecticides to kill mosquitoes, which can transmit malaria and yellow fever. By reducing populations of mosquitoes, these efforts reduced the spread of mosquito-borne illnesses. And advances in medical care in the early twentieth century reduced the risk of death for people who came down with most of the other infectious diseases.

But the most important advance in the fight against infectious diseases was the development of vaccines. Vaccines are pharmaceutical preparations that trigger the immune system to develop defenses against particular diseases. In the twentieth century, medical researchers developed vaccines for many infectious diseases. Health workers administered the vaccines—usually in the form of injections—to children and adults in the United States and around the world. Smallpox no longer kills anyone anywhere in the world since public health officials wiped it out through vaccination (also called inoculation). Polio exists in only a handful of countries. And neither measles nor rubella circulates regularly in North or South America thanks to vaccines. The US Centers for Disease Control and Prevention (CDC), a government health agency, ranks vaccination as the first of the top ten greatest health achievements of the twentieth century.

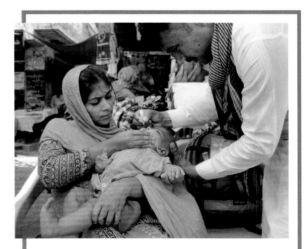

A health worker in Lahore, Pakistan, administers a polio vaccine to a baby in 2016. Thanks to global vaccination efforts, polio no longer circulates in most places on Earth. But it still circulates in Pakistan because of poverty, an underfunded healthcare system, and opposition to vaccination by some religious leaders.

That achievement has led to longer, healthier lives with less disability from vaccine-preventable diseases. Children in the United States, Canada, Australia, the nations of Europe, and most of the countries in Asia and Africa receive a recommended regime of vaccines starting in the first few months of life. Many teenagers receive several vaccines to protect them from diseases they might encounter as they enter early adulthood. Every year millions of people of all ages get vaccinated against influenza. As older adults age and their immune systems become weaker, they might get vaccines against shingles and pneumonia. Sometimes pregnant women get vaccines that protect their fetuses (developing babies) from diseases. And those who travel overseas might need vaccines before a trip to protect against diseases not present in their home countries. For instance, yellow fever is not found in the United States but is found in tropical parts of Africa and South America. So Americans who travel to these places must get yellow fever vaccinations before they leave home.

Humans have not conquered every infectious disease, and new ones are always appearing. For example, Zika virus is a tropical disease carried by mosquitoes that began to spread rapidly in 2015. Scientists are racing to develop a vaccine for that disease. Other scientists are committed to developing vaccines against malaria and dengue, which have plagued humanity for centuries and which still kill millions in poor nations. Still other scientists are working to develop a vaccine against human immunodeficiency virus (HIV), which scientists discovered in the 1980s to be the cause of acquired immunodeficiency syndrome (AIDS). HIV/AIDS kills more than one million people each year worldwide.

At the same time, public health officials must contend with another obstacle: public misunderstanding about and resistance to vaccination. Most people across the world recognize the value of preventing illness through vaccines, but others choose not to vaccinate themselves or their children. Some cite religious reasons for refusing vaccines. Others fear the side effects of vaccines. Still others don't

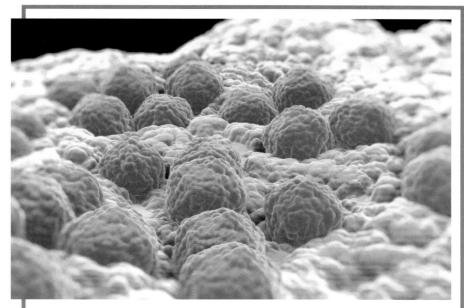

This photograph, shot through a high-powered microscope and colorized, shows rubella virus particles on the surface of human cells. When they enter the body, viruses, bacteria, and other pathogens (disease-carrying microbes) can lead to sickness and death. Vaccines prepare the immune system to fight off invading pathogens.

believe that infectious diseases are dangerous. They think it is "natural" to get a disease while it is "unnatural" to get a vaccination. But because diseases travel from one person to another, one person's refusal to vaccinate can affect others in the community. If someone fails to be vaccinated and gets sick, he or she can spread the disease to others who also aren't vaccinated. That makes widespread vaccination against disease a top public health priority.

THE IMMUNE SYSTEM: DEFENDING THE BODY

The body's immune system kicks into action when pathogens (disease-carrying microbes) enter the body. Perhaps an infected person accidentally sneezes on a healthy person, allowing germs to enter the healthy person's nose and mouth. What happens then?

Bacteria and viruses are two types of germs. Bacteria are one-celled microorganisms that have cell walls but lack the organ-like structures that most other cells have. Some bacteria benefit human health, while others cause disease. Viruses are microbes made of genetic material surrounded by a protein coat. Viruses can reproduce only inside a living cell. Bacteria and viruses both carry substances called antigens on their surfaces. An antigen is any protein, fat, or carbohydrate that the immune system can identify as foreign. When a pathogen enters the body, the immune system senses the presence of the antigens. It knows that the invader doesn't belong. After detecting the antigens, three types of immune cells that circulate in the body—macrophages, dendritic cells, and B cells—attack and devour some of the pathogens.

But the battle has just begun. That's because pathogens replicate, or reproduce, inside the body. So while the immune cells are devouring pathogens, other pathogens are replicating and continuing to attack the body.

At this point, the immune system gets even more organized. The immune cells that have devoured pathogens become antigen presenters. They display the antigens they have absorbed on their surfaces. They travel to the lymph nodes, bean-shaped organs found in many places in the body. In the lymph nodes, lots of immune cells gather, waiting for instructions from the immune system.

The antigen presenters show the antigens to the gathered immune cells. Seeing these antigens activates additional B cells, along with T cells and T-helper cells. Activation readies these cells to fight the specific pathogen that has invaded the body. Activated T-helper cells tell other B and T cells which pathogens to look for, training more immune cells to fight.

The immune system attacks the invader in several ways. Activated B cells become factories that produce and release hundreds of millions of tiny, Y-shaped proteins called antibodies. The antibodies are built to fit precisely onto the antigens of the invading pathogen. They swarm around bacterial cells or free-floating virus cells, latch onto their antigens, and deactivate the pathogen's ability to do harm and to reproduce.

Meanwhile, activated T cells become T-helper cells or a new type of cell called T-killer cells. In a bacterial infection, T-helper cells trigger other immune cells to kill the bacteria. During a viral infection, viruses enter the body's cells and hijack them, instructing the cells to create more viruses. T-killer cells look for antigens on hijacked body cells and destroy those cells.

While the immune cells are working together to defeat the infection, B cells, T cells, and T-helper cells also create memory cells. Their job is to remember the pathogen and how to fight it. The antibodies produced during the first battle with the infection are a standing army, ready to fight the invader if it returns. The person now has immunity from the disease. If it enters the body again, the memory cells and antibodies will kick in and defeat the pathogens even before symptoms develop.

VACCINES TRIGGER THE IMMUNE SYSTEM

Made from the same viruses or bacteria against which they defend, vaccines trick the immune system into thinking that an invader has arrived. They present the same antigens that trigger the cells of the immune system into action. But vaccines do not harm the body because they are made from weakened or killed viruses or bacteria. They trigger the immune system to prepare its defenses against a disease without the person having to endure the dangers of the real disease.

Essentially, a vaccination is similar to a fire drill. The whole school practices the procedures—from the alarm to the orderly evacuation of classes to lining up outside—that will be needed in the case of a real fire. If a real fire breaks out, everyone knows how to react safely and quickly. Similarly, a vaccine trains the immune system to fight a particular disease, but your body doesn't know it's a drill.

HOW THE IMMUNE SYSTEM WORKS

When a pathogen enters the body, certain immune cells attack and destroy it. Other immune cells remember the pathogen. They know how to defeat it if it enters the body again.

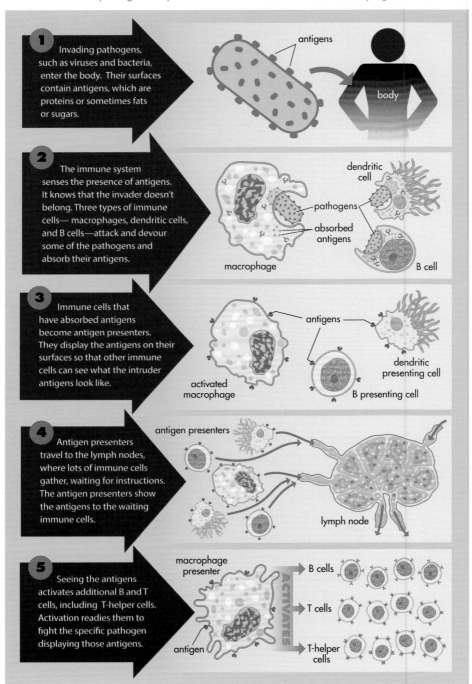

1 Invading pathogens, such as viruses and bacteria, enter the body. Their surfaces contain antigens, which are proteins or sometimes fats or sugars.

antigens

body

2 The immune system senses the presence of antigens. It knows that the invader doesn't belong. Three types of immune cells— macrophages, dendritic cells, and B cells—attack and devour some of the pathogens and absorb their antigens.

dendritic cell

pathogens

absorbed antigens

macrophage

B cell

3 Immune cells that have absorbed antigens become antigen presenters. They display the antigens on their surfaces so that other immune cells can see what the intruder antigens look like.

antigens

activated macrophage

dendritic presenting cell

B presenting cell

4 Antigen presenters travel to the lymph nodes, where lots of immune cells gather, waiting for instructions. The antigen presenters show the antigens to the waiting immune cells.

antigen presenters

lymph node

5 Seeing the antigens activates additional B and T cells, including T-helper cells. Activation readies them to fight the specific pathogen displaying those antigens.

macrophage presenter

ACTIVATES

B cells

T cells

T-helper cells

antigen

6 Activated T-helper cells help coordinate the rest of the immune system responses.

7 The immune system attacks the invader in several ways:

7a Activated B cells become factories that produce and release hundreds of millions of tiny proteins called antibodies. The antibodies are designed to fit precisely onto the antigens of the invading pathogen. They swarm bacterial cells or free-floating viruses, latch onto the antigens, and prevent the pathogen's ability to do harm.

7b Activated T cells can become T-helper cells or T-killer cells. T-helper cells trigger other immune cells to kill bacteria and body cells infected by viruses.

7c During viral infections, viruses enter the body's cells and hijack them, instructing the cells to create more viruses. The T-killer cells look for antigens on hijacked body cells and destroy them.

8 While the immune cells are working together to defeat the infection, B cells, T cells, and T-helper cells also create memory cells. Their job is to remember the pathogen and how to fight it. If the invader returns, the memory cells begin fighting it before the person even gets sick.

Images are not drawn to scale.

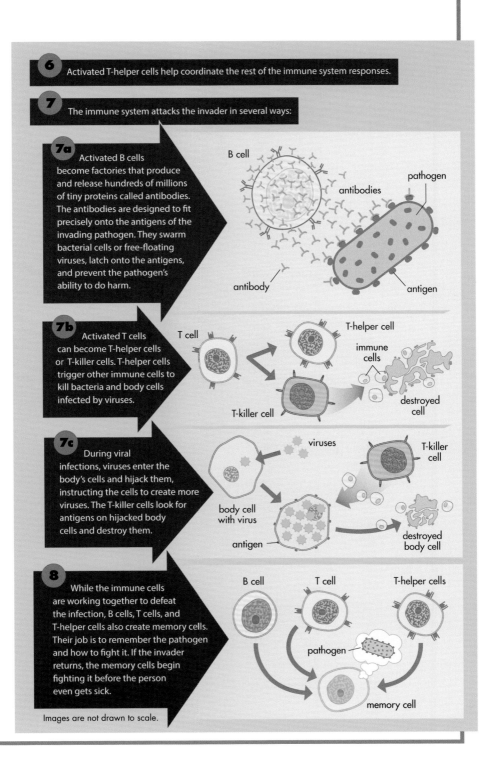

B cell
antibodies
pathogen
antibody
antigen

T cell
T-helper cell
immune cells
T-killer cell
destroyed cell

viruses
T-killer cell
body cell with virus
antigen
destroyed body cell

B cell
T cell
T-helper cells
pathogen
memory cell

Because it carries antigens, a vaccine tricks the immune system into thinking a real pathogen has entered the body. The immune system practices attacking the antigens and remembers how to fight them, a process called immunization. Vaccines are also called immunizations. If the real pathogen arrives, the immune cells respond more quickly and with more strength than they did when the vaccine first introduced the disease.

PROTECTING THE HERD

Vaccines train the body to fight disease at the individual level, while widespread vaccination creates immunity in an entire population. A disease can't spread very far in a community with high vaccination rates because only small numbers of people are vulnerable to the disease and pose a risk of passing it on to others.

Health officials say that a population with many vaccinated individuals has a high level of herd immunity, also called community immunity. Herd immunity is essential to prevent outbreaks and to shield unprotected people in a population from disease. For instance, if someone with measles enters a highly vaccinated population, one or two others might catch measles, but there won't be a major outbreak. The rest of the vaccinated "herd" protects those who are unvaccinated. Similarly, in a strategy called cocooning, vaccinating most members of a household helps protect any unvaccinated people in the household.

People might be unvaccinated for several reasons. Some are too young to get vaccinated. For instance, in the first two months of life, babies get only one vaccination, against hepatitis B. They are vulnerable to other diseases during these early months of life. Babies don't receive the measles-mumps-rubella (MMR) and chickenpox vaccines until they are twelve months old. If the children encounter these diseases before that, they might get sick. Elderly adults might be vulnerable to diseases for different reasons. For example, a medical condition, such as a severe allergy to a vaccine ingredient, might prevent an adult from

THE MOST FRIGHTENING MEASLES COMPLICATION

Measles causes death or brain damage in one or two of every one thousand cases. A much rarer complication, called subacute sclerosing panencephalitis (SSPE), occurs in about four to eleven of every one hundred thousand cases. SSPE causes the brain to deteriorate. But symptoms don't show up for six to eight years—sometimes even twenty to thirty years—after the measles infection.

The early symptoms of SSPE are memory loss, language loss, irritability, moodiness, and difficulty thinking. The symptoms become increasingly worse as the brain continues to deteriorate. Eventually the person enters a coma, where he or she might remain for years before dying. There is no cure or treatment for SSPE. Every case results in death, usually one to three years after diagnosis, although some patients remain in a coma-like state for ten years or longer.

"This is a puzzling disorder because it's apparent that the [measles] virus can persist in rare individuals in the brain or central nervous system and then slowly just be transferred from cell to cell," says Neal Halsey, a professor of global disease epidemiology and control at Johns Hopkins Bloomberg School of Public Health in Baltimore, Maryland.

Even though this fatal condition is very rare, doctors and public health officials point to it as an example of the importance of vaccination to prevent previously common infections such as measles.

getting a certain vaccine. Or a vaccine might not be effective because a disease such as AIDS or cancer, or chemotherapy treatment for cancer, has weakened the person's immune system. The immune system also simply becomes less effective as it ages.

Finally, some people might be unprotected and not know it. No vaccine protects 100 percent of those who receive it; some individuals don't respond to certain vaccines. The rotavirus vaccine is one example.

WHAT IS HERD IMMUNITY?

If only a few people in a community get vaccinated, disease easily spreads through the rest of the population. When most people are vaccinated, the spread of disease is very limited.

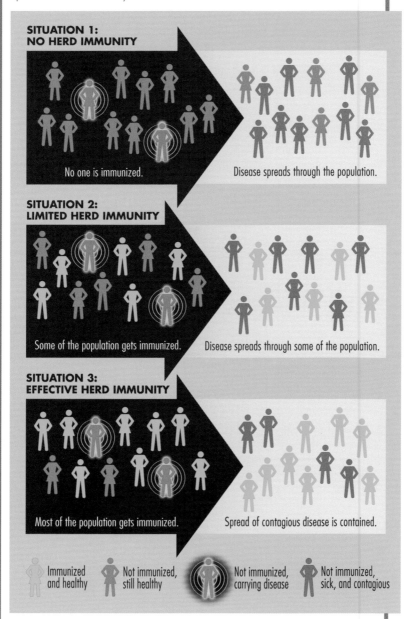

SITUATION 1:
NO HERD IMMUNITY

No one is immunized.

Disease spreads through the population.

SITUATION 2:
LIMITED HERD IMMUNITY

Some of the population gets immunized.

Disease spreads through some of the population.

SITUATION 3:
EFFECTIVE HERD IMMUNITY

Most of the population gets immunized.

Spread of contagious disease is contained.

Immunized and healthy

Not immunized, still healthy

Not immunized, carrying disease

Not immunized, sick, and contagious

It protects only 74 to 87 percent of the children who receive it. The pertussis vaccine is only 80 to 85 percent effective initially, and immunity wears off over time. Therefore, public health officials rely on herd immunity to protect the entire population, even if some members are not individually immune. If too many community members are not vaccinated, herd immunity breaks down, making it easier for a disease to infiltrate a population and sicken more people. The level of vaccination coverage required to maintain herd immunity varies for each disease.

WHAT'S IN A VACCINE?

The most important ingredients in a vaccine are antigens, the parts of a pathogen the immune system recognizes so that it can prime the body for future battles. To carry those antigens into the body, the vaccine might contain a virus or bacteria that has been weakened or inactivated, or it might carry just proteins from the pathogen. Vaccines also contain other ingredients to make them stable, safe, and effective.

To make a vaccine, scientists first grow a supply of the target virus or bacteria. To grow, viruses need a host to infect and bacteria need a nutrient-rich environment. These substances—for both viruses and bacteria—can include egg whites, chick embryos, insect cells, and human or bovine (cow) serum, a clear liquid that comes from blood. Bacteria and viruses also need nutrients, such as amino acids, bovine casein (a protein), sugars, carbohydrates, vitamins, and yeast. Tiny amounts of any of these substances may remain in the final vaccine formulation.

The major ingredients in a vaccine fall into several categories:

- Stabilizers, such as gelatin and sucrose (table sugar), keep all the ingredients in a vaccine mixed together and prevent ingredients from decomposing and becoming ineffective.
- Adjuvants, most commonly aluminum, boost the body's immune response to vaccines.

- Preservatives, such as thimerosal in the flu vaccine, prevent the growth of harmful fungi or new bacteria in vaccines.
- Antibiotics (drugs that kill or slow the growth of bacteria), often neomycin, also prevent new bacterial growth. Other antibiotics in vaccines include gentamicin, polymyxin, and streptomycin.
- Formaldehyde is used to inactivate the viruses and bacteria used during vaccine manufacturing. Trace amounts may remain in the final vaccine.

In very rare cases, one of these ingredients, usually egg white or gelatin, induces an allergic reaction in someone who receives a vaccine.

TYPES OF VACCINES

Not all pathogens behave the same way. So scientists have to design different types of vaccines to overcome the challenges of each bacteria or virus.

Live attenuated (weakened) vaccines are made of an attenuated form of a virus or live bacteria. Examples of live attenuated vaccines include the MMR, chickenpox, rotavirus, and shingles vaccines. One common method for attenuating a pathogen is to grow it in a nonhuman host generation after generation, so that it gets better and better at infecting that host. After many generations, often up to two hundred, the pathogen is very good at growing in the new host but is no longer able to replicate in a human. These pathogens still look like their full-strength versions to the human immune system and still stimulate an immune response, but they are too weak to cause harm. Live attenuated vaccines create the strongest immune response, but they also carry the highest risk of side effects. In extremely rare cases, some of these vaccines, such as the live polio vaccine, mutate (change form) inside the body. They revert to a form that can actually cause the disease.

Another type of vaccine is an inactivated vaccine. Examples of inactivated vaccines include the hepatitis A and rabies vaccines. Inactivated vaccines contain bacteria that have been killed or a virus that has been deactivated by the application of heat, radiation, or a chemical, such as formaldehyde. Inactivated pathogens cannot replicate inside the body. Since the pathogens in inactivated vaccines cannot multiply, these vaccines cannot cause disease. However, the immune system still recognizes the inactivated pathogens as invaders and responds. The response is usually weaker than with live vaccines, so individuals might need booster shots later in life to maintain immunity.

Toxoid vaccines are used when a toxin produced by bacteria, rather than the bacteria themselves, causes disease. Examples of toxoid vaccines are the diphtheria and tetanus vaccines. To make the vaccine, scientists deactivate the toxin to destroy the harmful parts, leaving behind a substance called a toxoid. When the immune system encounters a toxoid vaccine, it attacks the toxoid. The body's memory cells learn how to defend against the entire toxin.

Subunit vaccines include only certain pieces of a pathogen, usually proteins, since proteins are among the antigens that stimulate the immune system. Like inactivated vaccines, subunit vaccines do not cause disease, though they prompt the body to fight against the pathogen. Examples are some types of pertussis and influenza vaccines.

Recombinant vaccines are subunit vaccines made using genetic engineering. Examples of recombinant vaccines include the hepatitis B and human papillomavirus (HPV) vaccines. Genes are chemicals that carry instructions for how each living thing will grow, function, and reproduce. Genes are found on strands of deoxyribonucleic acid (DNA), chainlike molecules packed inside cells. To make recombinant vaccines, scientists take a gene that produces a certain protein from a disease-causing pathogen and insert it into a carrier virus. The carrier virus is harmless when it replicates inside the body. But it produces the protein from the disease-causing pathogen.

The immune system recognizes and attacks the protein.

Conjugate vaccines include the pneumococcal, *Haemophilus influenzae* type b (Hib), and meningitis vaccines. These are subunit vaccines used to defend against bacteria that camouflage themselves beneath coatings of polysaccharides (sugar molecules). The immature immune systems of babies and young children don't recognize the camouflage. To make conjugate vaccines, scientists attach the coating to an antigen, usually a protein, from a pathogen that the immune system does recognize. When it attacks the antigen, the immune system also attacks and remembers the coating.

DNA vaccines are the newest—and cleverest—type, but they are still experimental. DNA vaccines still in development include herpes and influenza vaccines. To create these vaccines, scientists analyze a pathogen's DNA to learn which genes carry instructions for making antigens. Scientists add the genes for specific antigens to a vaccine for a specific disease. When the DNA vaccine enters the human body, other

WHAT'S IN A NAME?

Scientists label every recognized species on Earth, including plants, animals, and bacteria, with a two-part scientific name. This system for naming species, called binomial nomenclature, was invented by Swedish botanist Carolus Linnaeus in the eighteenth century.

The first part of a scientific name, which is capitalized, labels a category called a genus. All organisms within a genus are closely related. Lions and tigers both belong to the genus *Panthera*. The second part of the scientific name, in lowercase, identifies the particular species to which an organism belongs, separate from all other species. Lions are the species *Panthera leo*. Tigers are *Panthera tigris*. Both parts of the scientific name are italicized.

Sometimes species names are abbreviated, with the genus indicated by only a capital letter. In this system *Clostridium tetani*, the bacteria that causes tetanus disease, is abbreviated as *C. tetani*.

kinds of cells (the type depends on the vaccine) pick up the genes and follow their instructions for making the antigens. The immune system then responds.

GENETIC ENGINEERING FOR VACCINES

Scientists use genetic engineering to make vaccines when traditional methods are not effective or safe. Genetic engineering involves intentionally modifying an organism's DNA to change its characteristics. Genetically engineered vaccines are called recombinant vaccines because scientists recombine genes to create substances to which the immune system will respond. The hepatitis B vaccine, introduced in the mid-1980s, was the first recombinant vaccine.

To make a recombinant vaccine, scientists remove parts of DNA from a pathogen and manipulate the DNA in a laboratory. They might remove genes, add genes, or modify a single gene. One common method involves inserting genes from a disease-causing pathogen into the DNA of a harmless "carrier agent." The carrier is often a virus that is naturally harmless or that scientists alter to make it harmless.

The genetically modified virus, which carries one or more of the pathogen's genes, is used as the vaccine. By itself, the virus does not cause harm in the person receiving the vaccine. However, the pathogen's genes inside the virus produce proteins that the person's immune system recognizes as foreign. The immune system creates antibodies against those proteins, providing immunity against the pathogen. If the vaccinated person later encounters that pathogen, the immune system attacks the pathogen before it makes the person sick.

A scientist at the National Institute of Allergy and Infectious Diseases works with genetic material in vaccine research.

VACCINE DELIVERY

Clinicians (nurses, doctors, and other health-care workers) deliver vaccines in one of five ways: orally, through the nose, and through three types of injections. Oral vaccines include the rotavirus vaccine, the live attenuated polio vaccine, and the live typhoid vaccine. The live flu vaccine, inhaled through a nostril, is a nasal vaccine.

One type of injection is intramuscular. For example, the hepatitis B and inactivated polio vaccines are injected into an arm or leg muscle. Subcutaneous vaccines, such as those against measles and yellow fever, are injected into the fatty layer between the skin and muscle. Intradermal vaccines, such as one of the inactivated flu vaccines, go only into the surface skin layer. Manufacturers sometimes combine multiple vaccines into one shot to reduce the number of injections the patient has to receive. Two combined vaccines used in the United States are the MMR and tetanus-diphtheria-pertussis (abbreviated as DTaP and Tdap) vaccines.

More options may exist in the future. Scientists are exploring the use of painless patches with extremely tiny needles that deliver intradermal vaccines into the skin. One type of patch dissolves after delivering the vaccine, similar to dissolving stitches. Some researchers are developing an oral vaccine contained on breath mint–type strips that dissolve on the tongue. Another area

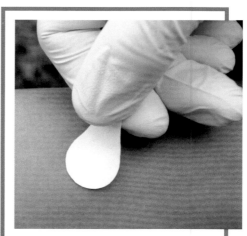

The underside of this small patch, developed by medical engineers at the Georgia Institute of Technology, contains microneedles that deliver vaccines into a patient's skin. The patient wears the patch for a few minutes—enough time for the skin to absorb the vaccine—and then peels it off. The patch is being tested on volunteers.

of exploration is edible vaccines. These are fruits or vegetables that have been genetically modified to produce proteins that can lead to a human immune response. Scientists have considered bananas, potatoes, tomatoes, lettuce, rice, wheat, soybeans, and corn for use as edible vaccines, but research is still in the very early stages.

THE CDC IMMUNIZATION SCHEDULE

The Advisory Committee on Immunization Practices (ACIP) at the CDC in Atlanta, Georgia, issues a recommended vaccination schedule for individuals. The committee is made up of researchers, physicians, and other experts. It meets twice a year to review evidence about the effectiveness of certain vaccines and to recommend changes to the vaccination schedule.

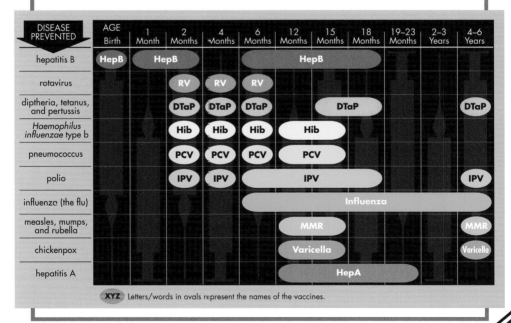

THE CDC'S RECOMMENDED VACCINATION SCHEDULE FOR CHILDREN

The US Centers for Disease Control and Prevention recommends a schedule of vaccines for babies and young children. The schedule calls for varying doses of different vaccines.

DISEASE PREVENTED	AGE Birth	1 Month	2 Months	4 Months	6 Months	12 Months	15 Months	18 Months	19–23 Months	2–3 Years	4–6 Years
hepatitis B	HepB	HepB				HepB					
rotavirus			RV	RV	RV						
diptheria, tetanus, and pertussis			DTaP	DTaP	DTaP		DTaP				DTaP
Haemophilus influenzae type b			Hib	Hib	Hib	Hib					
pneumococcus			PCV	PCV	PCV	PCV					
polio			IPV	IPV	IPV						IPV
influenza (the flu)					Influenza						
measles, mumps, and rubella						MMR					MMR
chickenpox						Varicella					Varicella
hepatitis A						HepA					

XYZ Letters/words in ovals represent the names of the vaccines.

The CDC advises that children from birth to the age of six get various doses of nine vaccines, for a total of approximately twenty-eight doses. Those doses protect children against thirteen diseases that can cause death or serious disability: hepatitis B, rotavirus, diphtheria, tetanus, pertussis, Hib, pneumococcal disease, polio, measles, mumps, rubella, chickenpox, and hepatitis A. Six more doses over six years (one per year) protect children against influenza as well.

At first glance, the CDC's vaccine recommendations can seem intimidating. Some parents feel overwhelmed by the schedule and worry whether their children's immune systems can handle what the schedule recommends. However, CDC recommendations rely on hundreds, even thousands of rigorous studies. They have all determined the vaccines to be safe and have identified the ideal time for children to receive them.

VACCINES FOR TEENS

The CDC immunization schedule recommends vaccines for preteens and teenagers as well as for babies. The three vaccines recommended for all teenagers are the HPV vaccine, a booster dose of the Tdap vaccine, and a vaccine that protects against meningococcal disease, which is caused by four types of the *Neisseria meningitidis* bacteria. Meningococcal disease can cause infection in the bloodstream or the brain and spinal cord. About 10 to 15 percent of those who develop this infection will die. About 11 to 19 percent of the survivors have severe disabilities, such as brain damage, damaged limbs requiring amputation, or deafness. The CDC also recommends that teens and their parents should talk to a doctor about an optional vaccine against a fifth type of meningococcal disease called serotype B.

02

VACCINE HISTORY

In the twenty-first century, scientists know that germs—viruses, bacteria, parasites, and fungi—can cause disease. This concept is called germ theory. Some germs travel by air, so a sick person can infect others simply by sharing breathing space. Other germs need bodily fluids, such as saliva, blood, tears, or semen, to survive. The germs can pass between individuals when one person comes into contact with infected fluid from another person, such as through open wounds, sex, or sneezing.

But even before humans discovered germs or knew about germ theory (which was proved in the nineteenth

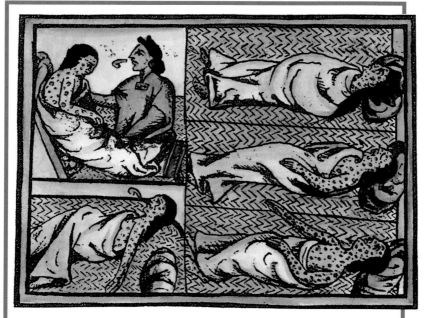

When Europeans infected with smallpox came to the Americas, starting in the late fifteenth century, they spread the virus to American Indians. The Indians had no natural immunity to smallpox, and the deadly disease spread rapidly. In the sixteenth century, Spaniard Bernardino de Sahagún wrote the *Florentine Codex*, a chronicle of life and culture in Mesoamerica (lands that became Mexico). This illustration from the codex shows Indians dying of smallpox. The black dots on their bodies represent smallpox blisters.

century), some noticed that those who got sick with certain diseases and recovered never got sick with those diseases again. One of the most frightening of these diseases was smallpox, a virus that enters the body through the lungs. Smallpox causes severe blistering on the skin that leaves disfiguring pockmarks. The virus sometimes attacks the eyes, leading to blindness. It can also damage the limbs. Historically, most children who got smallpox died.

Doctors and researchers eradicated smallpox in the late twentieth century, but for thousands of years, humans feared the terrible disease. Symptoms started with a high fever one to two weeks after exposure to the virus. Next came headaches, body aches, swollen eyes, nausea, and vomiting. The victim was most contagious when a rash of tissue-filled pimples broke out a few days later. These blisters slowly leaked pus that then crusted and scabbed over. The person remained infectious until the last scab fell off, usually three weeks later. In the twentieth century, doctors who studied the mummy of the ancient Egyptian pharaoh Ramses V concluded that the lesions on his face were likely caused by smallpox. Scientists believe that smallpox probably developed around 10,000 BCE in northeastern Africa and from there spread to the Middle East, Europe, and Asia.

Of the four types of smallpox, two were nearly always fatal. A third type, called variola major, killed about 30 percent of the people who caught it. This was the most common form of the disease. The fourth type was variola minor. It killed only 1 percent of people who caught it.

About 1000 BCE, doctors in China and India noted that those who survived smallpox of any type seemed to be immune to the disease after that. So doctors and other healers began intentionally infecting patients with variola minor, believing they could prevent major infections later. This process is called variolation. Practitioners took dried pox scabs from people with a mild smallpox infection and ground the scabs into a powder. In China, doctors gave the powder to patients to inhale it through a tube. In India, healers rubbed the powder into scratches in patients' skin. In northeastern Africa, the Sudanese wrapped smallpox-infected cloths around children's scratched arms. A person infected through variolation would experience mild smallpox symptoms for two to four weeks, but the disease usually didn't kill or scar the person.

WIDESPREAD AND DEADLY

In the Middle Ages in Europe (about 500–1500), smallpox was a major killer. Starting in the late fifteenth century, European explorers spread the disease to the Americas, where it had never appeared before. Because smallpox was completely new to them, no American Indians had immunity to it. Initially, the disease spread naturally among American

Indians. But sometimes Europeans tried to deliberately infect native peoples with smallpox to kill them, or they threatened to spread the disease if native peoples did not concede to European demands for land or peace.

The virus wiped out entire peoples in some regions. In lands that later became Mexico, smallpox slashed the Aztec population from twenty-five million in 1519 to three million just fifty years later. In territory that became the southeastern United States, the disease killed between seven thousand and ten thousand Cherokees—half the tribal population—in 1738 and 1739.

Back in Europe, an estimated four hundred thousand Europeans died every year from smallpox in the eighteenth century. Lady Mary Wortley Montagu was married to the British ambassador to the Ottoman Empire, a political power based in lands that later became Turkey. In 1717 she, her husband, and their five-year-old son traveled to Constantinople (modern-day Istanbul, Turkey), where her husband had business. There, Lady Montagu observed doctors performing variolation. She had been scarred by smallpox herself and her brother had died of smallpox. She wanted to protect her children from the disease, so she had a doctor variolate her son in Turkey. When she returned to Great Britain, another doctor variolated her four-year-old daughter. British officials were eager to test the procedure to see if it could save lives. They offered pardons to six death-row prisoners if they would agree to be variolated. The prisoners underwent variolation, and when some of them were later exposed to smallpox, they did not get sick. This experiment convinced more doctors and government officials that variolation was effective.

In the early eighteenth century, in the North American colony of Massachusetts, Puritan minister Cotton Mather learned about variolation from a slave named Onesimus, who had been variolated in Africa as a child. When smallpox arrived in Boston, Massachusetts, on a ship in April 1721, it quickly became an epidemic—a sudden outbreak of disease with many more cases than would occur normally in the population. Mather successfully convinced a Boston doctor to treat 242 citizens with variolation. Many other doctors in the city opposed it, partly because of concerns about safety and partly because they considered it abhorrent to intentionally infect a healthy person with a disease. By the time the epidemic ended in December, only 6 of the 242 variolated patients (2.5 percent) had died. In contrast, 849 of the 5,889 citizens with naturally occurring smallpox infections (15 percent) had died. The statistics helped convince doctors and the public that variolation was effective. George Washington—then head of American forces fighting for independence from Great Britain—knew of the success in fighting smallpox. He required all his troops to be variolated.

JENNER'S EXPERIMENT

Variolation was not without risk. Some who were variolated still died during smallpox epidemics. Edward Jenner (1749–1823), a British doctor, discovered a safer way to protect people from smallpox. As a young apprentice to a surgeon, he had heard a milkmaid say that those who caught cowpox, a disease that mostly infected cows, were protected from smallpox. That belief was common among milkmaids.

Once Jenner was an established physician, he decided to test the milkmaids' claim scientifically. He infected his ten-month-old son with swinepox, very similar to cowpox, from the boy's nurse. When he then variolated the boy with smallpox, no infection developed. For another ten years, Jenner studied others who contracted cowpox and afterward seemed immune to smallpox. Then, on May 14, 1796, Jenner did a public experiment. He took cowpox pus from a blister on the hand of milkmaid Sarah Nelms. With permission, he made a cut on the arm of his gardener's son, eight-year-old James Phipps, and infected it with the pus. James developed a mild fever that lasted for a few days and a blister that healed two weeks later. Jenner later infected James with pus from a fresh smallpox blister, but the boy did not get smallpox.

PATHOGENS THAT JUMP SPECIES

Some viruses, called zoonotic viruses, naturally infect both humans and other types of animals. Examples are type A influenza viruses. Other diseases mostly infect specific animals but have the potential to mutate and infect humans. If a human comes into close contact with an infected animal or consumes the raw meat of one, the pathogen may mutate into a slightly different genetic form inside the human and thereby "jump" to a human population. Scientists call this process spillover.

Zika and HIV originally infected monkeys or apes. Middle East respiratory syndrome (MERS) and severe acute respiratory syndrome (SARS) also likely came from animals—MERS from camels and SARS possibly from catlike mammals called civets. When an infection breaks out in a population of animals living close to humans, scientists monitor the disease closely to contain the spillover.

Recent analyses of smallpox DNA suggest that two forms of the disease might have evolved from a similar virus in African rodents between sixteen thousand and sixty-eight thousand years ago. If that's true, then smallpox was originally zoonotic. By the time humans first wrote about the disease, however, in the fourth century CE, it infected only humans and was therefore no longer zoonotic.

Others, such as a farmer named Benjamin Jesty, had done similar experiments before Jenner, but Jenner was the first to publish a paper on his experiment. He called his procedure vaccination, for *vaccinia*, the scientific word for cowpox. (*Vacca* is Latin for "cow.")

Vaccination soon became common practice in Great Britain. As news of Jenner's success spread to the United States, vaccination became common there too. In 1806 US president Thomas Jefferson wrote to Jenner, "It is owing to your discovery . . . that in the future the

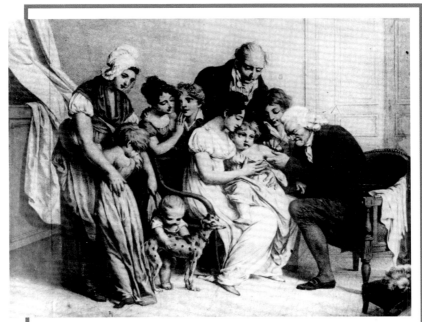

This nineteenth-century illustration shows Edward Jenner infecting his infant son with swinepox. That infection served to inoculate the boy from smallpox. The experiment was the first step in Jenner's development of a smallpox vaccine.

peoples of the world will learn about this disgusting smallpox disease only from ancient traditions"

THE NEXT BIG KILLER

Medical science took a great step forward in the late nineteenth century when French chemist Louis Pasteur and German physician Robert Koch established the germ theory of disease. Pasteur figured out that bacteria cause wine to spoil, and he believed that bacteria could also cause disease. Koch deliberately infected animals with pathogens, observing that the animals then became sick.

Pasteur developed the world's next two vaccines. The first prevented cholera in chickens, and the second prevented rabies in humans. The definition of *vaccination*—which originally referred to inducing immunity against only smallpox—expanded to refer to immunization against other infectious diseases.

In Europe and the United States, vaccination led to a dwindling number of smallpox cases. But in the early twentieth century, polio began to increase in the United States. Poliovirus, the pathogen responsible for the disease, had been around since ancient times. Yet for thousands of years, the virus did not cause severe, widespread disease. Poliovirus exists in water. In the centuries before public sanitation systems and indoor plumbing, most infants were exposed to the virus early in life through unclean water. Infants who are exposed to poliovirus usually experience no symptoms and develop immunity against polio. But those who don't encounter the virus until later in childhood or adulthood can get extremely sick. Polio can cause permanent muscle pain, weakness, and stiffness. If the virus travels to the spinal cord, it can cause paralysis of some or all of the body. Some patients with paralyzed upper bodies die because they can't breathe.

As clean water became more common in the United States, infants were no longer regularly exposed to polio and therefore did not develop immunity naturally. This made them vulnerable to the disease if they later encountered it as children or adults. In one of the worst polio epidemics ever recorded, during the summer of 1916 in New York City, the virus killed 2,243 and paralyzed more than 9,300 others, mostly under the age of ten. The development of the iron lung in 1928 helped paralyzed patients continue breathing and prevented many polio deaths.

Polio was especially difficult to fight because 95 percent of those who are infected have no symptoms at all, but they still carry the virus and can transmit it to others. It therefore was impossible to know who was infected and contagious unless they developed symptoms. This also made it difficult to know whom to quarantine (isolate to keep them from infecting others), since there was no way to identify everyone who was infected. "People were terrified," explained Peter Salk, whose father, Jonas Salk, eventually developed a polio vaccine. "This disease struck without warning, and there was no way of predicting who was going to get it and who wasn't."

Researchers worked desperately to develop a polio vaccine, but their first attempts ended in failure. President Franklin D. Roosevelt—himself paralyzed from the waist down by polio—made developing a vaccine a top priority. In 1938 he launched the National Foundation for Infantile Paralysis, later renamed the March of Dimes, to raise money for research. (That's why Roosevelt is featured on the US dime.)

Polio struck Franklin D. Roosevelt in 1921, eleven years before he was elected president of the United States. The disease left him almost completely paralyzed below the waist. He could walk only with the help of heavy leg braces, and he often used a wheelchair to move from place to place. He is pictured here with the granddaughter of a household staff person in 1941.

In 1952 polio reached its US peak with the worst epidemic in the nation's history, involving 57,628 cases and 3,145 deaths. That same year, after four years of work, US physician Jonas Salk developed an experimental vaccine covering all three strains of polio. With funding from the National Foundation for Infantile Paralysis, Salk tested his vaccine from May 1953 through March 1954. He administered the vaccine to more than 5,300 volunteers, including himself, his wife,

In a testing program in 1953 and 1954, more than five thousand volunteers received Jonas Salk's polio vaccine. In this image from 1953, Salk himself administers the vaccine to a young Polio Pioneer.

and his three sons. No one who was vaccinated suffered serious side effects, and tests showed anti-polio antibodies in the blood of all the volunteers. After that success, the foundation began the largest vaccine trial in history, costing $7.5 million and funded entirely by private donations. For the trial, more than 250,000 volunteer health workers vaccinated the "Polio Pioneers," more than 1.8 million first, second, and third graders in forty-four states.

On April 12, 1955, Thomas Francis Jr., the chair of the University of Michigan Department of Epidemiology, declared that Salk's polio vaccine was "safe, effective and potent," with 80 to 90 percent effectiveness. According to Salk biographer David Oshinsky, "People were hugging in the streets, kids were let out of school, Salk was invited to the White House where [President Dwight] Eisenhower broke down in tears thanking him—it was really this shining moment of great faith in science and in medical research." Between 1955 and 1962, health-care workers administered about four hundred million doses of Salk's vaccine across the United States. In that period, US polio rates dropped 96 percent.

DISASTER FOLLOWS TRIUMPH

In the wake of development of the polio vaccine—one of public health's greatest achievements—the United States suffered one of its greatest public health disasters. A one-year-old boy received the polio vaccine in April 1955, right after it became available, and eight days later, he was completely paralyzed. More cases of paralysis soon appeared, all in children who had received polio vaccines manufactured at Cutter Laboratories in Berkeley, California.

Cutter was one of five companies licensed by the federal government to produce the polio vaccine in April 1955. But because of the urgency of getting children vaccinated, the licensing process was the fastest in history for a vaccine. The US government approved the five licenses only two and a half hours after the inactivated vaccine was announced to be safe and effective. Of the first thirteen lots of polio vaccine distributed, six were from Cutter. Within forty-eight hours of news of the first paralysis case, Cutter recalled its vaccine from distributors. But by then, nearly four hundred thousand Americans, mostly children, had already received Cutter's vaccine.

Testing revealed that one of every three Cutter vaccines contained live instead of inactivated viruses. The Cutter vaccines ended up paralyzing fifty-one children and killing five. Even worse, the vaccine-caused polio was contagious, setting off an epidemic that paralyzed another 113 people and killed an additional 5.

WHAT WENT WRONG?

Because of low-quality lab equipment, formaldehyde for killing the virus didn't inactivate all the viruses used to make the vaccine during the manufacturing process. The company tested the vaccine on monkeys, but the tests were not sensitive enough to detect the live virus in their bodies. The vaccine also contained an especially powerful strain of poliovirus, which led to a stronger immune response but also caused more paralysis. Later that year, health officials discovered that another drug company, Wyeth, had also produced polio vaccines with a live virus. Those vaccines likely caused another eleven paralysis cases. After the disaster, the US government tightened its regulations about vaccine licensing, and manufacturers strengthened their safety procedures.

GOING GLOBAL WITH THE POLIO VACCINE

Jonas Salk's polio vaccine was an inactivated vaccine. At Cincinnati Children's Hospital in Ohio, Dr. Albert Sabin developed a live polio vaccine and tested it in Eastern Europe, Asia, and Latin America from 1957 to 1959. The Food and Drug Administration (FDA), a US government agency that regulates medications and medical devices, licensed four different formulations of the vaccine in 1961 and 1962.

Sabin's vaccine was not as safe as Salk's. It caused paralytic polio in one of every 2.7 million people who received a dose. But it was cheaper than Salk's vaccine. In addition, Salk's vaccine had to be administered with an injection, whereas Sabin's was administered orally, with just two drops of liquid in the mouth. Even people without medical training could give the live vaccine. These advantages made Sabin's vaccine a better choice for polio immunization on a grand scale around the world.

The last US polio case occurred in 1979. In 1988 the World Health Organization (WHO)—an international agency in Geneva, Switzerland, that develops policies and programs to improve people's health worldwide—began a campaign to eradicate the disease around the world. With this vaccination effort, the WHO certified North and South America free from polio in 1994, followed by Australia and much of Asia in 2000. Europe followed in 2002 and Southeast Asia in 2014.

The original WHO goal for eradication of polio was the year 2000. By that year, the annual number of polio infections had dropped 90 percent since 1988. But polio is not yet entirely gone from Earth. It still occurs in Afghanistan, Nigeria, and Pakistan. In 2014 it reappeared in Syria, where civil war was raging and vaccination efforts fell apart in the chaos. Polio could also return in several other countries where it has already been wiped out if people who don't know they are infected travel there. If someone infected with polio arrives in an area without the disease but also without widespread immunization against it, that one infection could reintroduce the disease to the region.

ERADICATION OF SMALLPOX

Thanks to vaccination, the last US smallpox case occurred in 1949. Vaccination wiped out smallpox in Europe and East Asia in the following decades. But elsewhere, the disease still circulated. In 1967 smallpox infected fifteen million people globally and killed two million of them. At the start of 1967, WHO kicked off its Intensified Smallpox Eradication Programme, designed to wipe out smallpox completely. US doctor and epidemiologist Donald A. Henderson led the effort.

A smallpox rash is unmistakable, which makes it easy to identify someone with the disease. That was essential to the eradication effort because it enabled WHO workers to easily identify those who had been infected and quickly vaccinate those they regularly came in contact with. The program was a success. By the 1970s, smallpox was gone from India and central Asia.

On October 26, 1977, twenty-three-year-old hospital cook Ali Maow Maalin, in the East African nation of Somalia, was found to have smallpox. In just two weeks, WHO workers tracked down and vaccinated 54,777 people who may have been exposed to his infection. Maalin was the last person on Earth known to have smallpox.

Exactly two years after the Maalin case appeared, on October 26, 1979, the WHO director general announced in Nairobi, Kenya, that smallpox was gone for good. The disease has been eradicated in nature, although many laboratories still have stocks of smallpox virus. (For decades, scientists have debated whether to destroy the samples or not. Some experts worry that terrorists will release illegal supplies of smallpox to harm certain groups. If that were to happen, officials would need a supply to create vaccines to protect targeted populations.) Maalin, meanwhile, lived until 2013, when he died from malaria. He had spent the last decade of his life working with health officials to vaccinate Somalis against polio.

The last person known to have smallpox was Somali Ali Maow Maalin, who contracted the disease in 1977 and survived. As evident in this undated photo, the disease left pockmarks on Maalin's body.

GLOBAL VACCINE CHALLENGES

In the twenty-first century, WHO runs vaccination programs around the world for many different diseases. A major challenge of distributing vaccines worldwide is maintaining an effective "cold chain." That means keeping vaccines at the appropriate temperature during their journey—from the manufacturer to the person ultimately receiving the vaccine. Most vaccines must be refrigerated at temperatures between 35°F and 46°F (2°C and 8°C). If vaccines freeze or get too warm, they can become ineffective or even dangerous. Vaccines usually start the journey to their destination in refrigerated containers on ships and trucks. In poor nations, many villages are hard to reach. They aren't connected to a network of paved roads. To reach remote communities, vaccinators (health-care workers who vaccinate people) often have to travel by bicycle or on foot. In those cases, they carry vaccines in insulated coolers.

Warfare can make delivering vaccines even more difficult. Many families around the world live in active, dangerous war zones. Others,

Health workers carrying vaccines in coolers arrive in a Ugandan village after a two-hour drive and 1.3-mile (2 km) hike. The village is far from any health clinics or hospitals, so residents can't easily take their children for vaccinations. Instead, health workers bring vaccines to the village.

fleeing war, live in refugee camps. Sona Bari, a spokesperson for WHO's Global Polio Eradication Initiative, explains that it's difficult to deliver vaccines to children in these places. "It's very hard to reach children in remote areas, in areas where there's [political and economic] insecurity, and these are some of the most dangerous places in the world," she says. "How do we reach those children who live by the side of the road, who might be in transit on buses, who are children of migrants that don't get any health services?"

Vaccine shortages pose another logistical challenge, particularly during unexpected outbreaks of disease. That happened in 2016 when the largest outbreak of yellow fever in thirty years hit Angola and the Democratic Republic of the Congo in Africa. Yellow fever no longer occurs in most of the world, so few companies make a yellow fever vaccine. International vaccinators quickly went through an emergency stockpile of six million doses of vaccine. After that, vaccinators were forced to give each recipient only one-fifth of a regular dose, which provided protection for one year instead of the ten years' protection provided by a full dose. Before the outbreak ended late in the year, an estimated four hundred people had died.

In many nations, vaccinators have also faced resistance, including violence. In Pakistan, for instance, leaders of a political group called the Taliban became suspicious of WHO vaccinators—and for good reason. In 2010 the US Central Intelligence Agency (CIA), the nation's spy agency, wanted to verify the location of Osama bin Laden. He was the mastermind behind the September 11, 2001, terrorist attacks in the United States, which had killed nearly three thousand people. The CIA suspected that bin Laden lived with his family in a home in Abbottabad, Pakistan. To confirm this, the CIA had a plan for health workers there to collect a little blood from children in the home while they were being vaccinated for hepatitis B. Technicians would then secretly analyze DNA from the blood and compare it to samples on file from other bin Laden family members. Those in the same family have similar DNA, so the analysis would help confirm that the children were bin Laden's offspring. If so, the CIA believed it was likely he was living in the same house with them. Then the US military could raid the house and capture or kill bin Laden. The vaccination plot fell apart, so US spies used other methods to confirm that bin Laden was living in the house. US Navy SEALs eventually raided the home and shot and killed bin Laden there in May 2011.

After news of the vaccination scheme broke, public health officials worldwide condemned it. They believed that it harmed international vaccination and health efforts and destroyed trust in local health-care workers. At the same time, the Taliban banned vaccinations in Pakistan, convinced that all vaccinators were US spies. Since December 2012, Taliban operatives have murdered about eighty vaccinators in Pakistan or those trying to protect them. Vaccinators have been shot, attacked by dogs, and splashed with gasoline and set on fire.

In February 2013, similar killings started in Nigeria, where religious leaders had distrusted the safety of vaccines for a decade. In 2003 political and religious leaders encouraged residents of three northern Nigerian states—Kano, Zamfara, and Kaduna—to refuse polio vaccinations. They feared that vaccines from Western, developed nations could cause HIV, cancer, or infertility. A doctor in Kano told a South African newspaper, "We believe that modern-day Hitlers [a reference to German dictator Adolf Hitler, who ordered the killing of six million Jews and others during World War II (1939–1945)] have deliberately adulterated the oral polio vaccines with anti-fertility drugs and . . . viruses which are known to cause HIV and AIDS."

The vaccination boycott in Nigeria lasted eleven months. After meetings with representatives of WHO, the United Nations Children's Fund (UNICEF), and the Nigerian government, local leaders agreed to resume vaccinations in July 2004. But the boycott took its toll. From 2003 through 2006, the number of polio cases in Nigeria multiplied five times.

The violence has interrupted WHO's polio eradication initiative, and polio has increased in some areas as a result. Fearing for their safety, some vaccinators have stopped working, but others continue, despite the danger and extremely low pay. "The real heroes of this campaign are the vaccinators who keep doing their jobs in high-risk areas without fear," says Elias Durry, head of the Global Polio Eradication Initiative. "They are not soldiers who are trained to battle. They are just there to do the right thing."

Sona Bari stresses that the vaccination effort must continue, despite resistance. "If we don't snuff [polio] out now when it's in these tiny, tiny areas, it's going to come back," she says. "We can't let a child on the border of Pakistan and Afghanistan be less protected than a child in Switzerland. It's a moral imperative."

ERADICATION VERSUS ELIMINATION

Eradication of a disease and elimination of a disease are not the same thing. Eradicating a disease means removing it completely from Earth. After eradication, no one anywhere can become infected with it.

Public health officials try to achieve eradication by first controlling a disease. They reduce new cases (the incidence) and existing cases (the prevalence) of the disease. When incidence is zero in a country or geographical region, the disease has been eliminated there. Elimination means the disease is no longer endemic, or circulating on its own throughout a geographical area. If an infected person enters that area from outside, public health officials must control the outbreak. If they do, the disease is still considered eliminated from that area. Public officials can declare a disease eradicated only after it has been eliminated from all geographical regions in the world for at least two to three years.

Not many diseases can be eradicated. Health officials must have an effective way to interrupt transmission, usually a vaccine, and must be able to accurately identify, diagnose, and track infections. That was easy with smallpox but has been more difficult with polio. The disease must also live only in human hosts, not other animals or the environment, or else it could reinfect humans even after being eliminated. If a disease meets these criteria, nations must commit enough money, resources, and political support to carry out the eradication effort. Measles, mumps, and rubella are among the handful of diseases that meet these requirements.

03

CREATING A VACCINE

It's no small task to develop a vaccine.
Vaccinologists start by examining the microbe itself. How does it attack the body? How does the immune system fight back? How can vaccinologists prepare the immune system to battle this particular microbe?

Every pathogen presents a different puzzle to solve. Scientists must study every piece of an organism—whether it is a virus, a parasite, a bacterium, or a toxin emitted by bacteria. They look at the parts of the pathogen that interact with the human immune system. Then they have to figure out how to use some piece of the pathogen, or how to combine it with other substances, to trick the immune system into thinking it is a real invader that needs to be attacked.

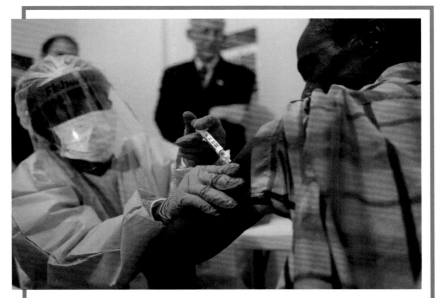

In 2015, at the height of an Ebola outbreak in West Africa, the US National Institutes of Health and the Liberian Ministry of Health developed an Ebola vaccine and tested it on volunteers. Here, a nurse administers the vaccine at Redemption Hospital in Monrovia, Liberia.

"The fact that viruses and bacteria work in different ways and the immune responses that protect against them are not all the same means there's no general solution to developing a vaccine," explains vaccinologist Stanley Plotkin, a former pediatrics professor at the University of Pennsylvania and head of the company Vaxconsult LLC. "One has to understand the biology of the organism and do a lot of experiments in animals before even considering going into humans, because one needs some evidence that the vaccine will be safe and some reason to believe it will work."

According to Michael Shea, a vaccine researcher at the University of Oxford in Great Britain, 'Four criteria must be met if a vaccine is to be effective: the immune system must be able to generate an effective response; the response must cover all major strains of a pathogen; the vaccine must be produced cheaply and efficiently; and the side effects must be small enough to be accepted by the public."

Two key resources are essential: time and money. First, scientists at universities, government agencies, and pharmaceutical companies research pathogens in the laboratory for several years or sometimes decades. They experiment to learn what kind of vaccine might work best on a certain pathogen. They develop multiple potential vaccines. They test them on laboratory animals, such as monkeys, to get an idea of how the vaccines might behave in humans and to determine safe dosages. If a vaccine seems promising, researchers conduct a series of trials, or tests, in which groups of human volunteers receive the vaccine. Universities and other research institutions oversee the trials. Private organizations, government agencies, and pharmaceutical companies fund this research. If the trials show the vaccine to be safe and effective, the FDA (or a similar organization in another country) will license the vaccine. This FDA approval allows a pharmaceutical company to produce and sell the vaccine.

Plotkin estimates that the fastest time frame for vaccine development and licensing is around seven years. Many vaccines take much longer—up to twenty years. And it costs between $500 million and $1 billion to develop and license a vaccine for use.

Then there is the human element. Vaccinologists must be prepared for the lengthy, grueling job of developing a vaccine. "One has to be a pessimist in the laboratory but an optimist overall," Plotkin explains. "You have to be very self-critical about what you do and what you make—you have to always look for faults [in a vaccine]—but on the other hand, if you're not an optimist, you shouldn't go into vaccine development because it's a long haul, and immediate gratification is not part of it."

Vaccinologists work long hours—and sometimes the payoff never comes. Since the early twentieth century, development on hundreds of vaccines has begun but stalled or been abandoned.

ANIMAL TESTING IN VACCINES

Before any vaccine trials with humans, scientists test vaccines on animals. Because the bodies of nonhuman primates (such as monkeys and apes) are similar to those of humans, researchers often use them for vaccine tests. Macaque monkeys are the most commonly used animals in vaccine testing. Scientists also use mice, rats, rabbits, sheep, pigs, cows, horses (very rarely), and other monkey types. For scientific research in general, about 95 percent of all lab animals are rodents. About 0.3 percent are nonhuman primates.

Using animals for scientific research is controversial. Many people believe it is unethical and cruel. Laws regarding the treatment of research animals have become stricter over the years, and several European countries have banned the use of certain animals, especially primates.

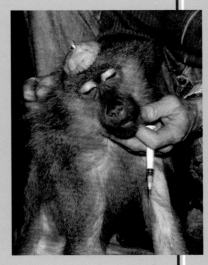

In the United States, an animal rights group called People for the Ethical Treatment of Animals (PETA) has called for an end to animal testing. Pressured by PETA, the NIH—the nation's largest government medical research center—announced in 2015 that all existing research chimpanzees (a type of ape) would immediately be retired to a sanctuary. The institution will no longer support research in chimpanzees. Research using other types of primates continues, however.

Animal rights activists decry experiments such as this one, which involves cutting open the skulls of monkeys and baboons to study epilepsy in humans. Vaccine testing also involves animal experimentation.

PHASE I, II, AND III TESTING

Testing of new vaccines and drugs involves several phases of study. Phase I trials are very small, usually involving twenty to one hundred participants. These tests evaluate a drug or vaccine's safety and dosage. The participants are either healthy (in the case of vaccines) or have the disease the drug is supposed to treat. They are often paid for their involvement. One group of volunteers is given the vaccine, and the other is given a placebo (fake vaccine) so that scientists can compare the groups. Larger Phase II trials involve up to several hundred volunteers and focus on the drug's efficacy (the power to produce results) and side effects. Phase III trials involve hundreds to thousands of participants and further assess how well the drug or vaccine works. Phase III studies also look for side effects too rare to detect in smaller trials.

Participants in all trials must provide informed consent: they must agree in writing to participate after being fully informed of the trial's purpose, its procedures, and all the risks, benefits, and side effects that might occur. They can ask questions at any time during the trial and can stop participating at any time.

The US Department of Health and Human Services (HHS) has specific requirements for research involving US children. All trials require the informed consent of one or both parents or guardians. When possible, the child's assent (agreement to participate) is required if the child is old enough, mature enough, and healthy enough to provide consent.

Only a tiny percentage of drugs make it out of Phase III to be licensed. After licensure by the FDA, additional Phase IV studies assess the product in the general population. The goal in these studies is to compare the drug to other similar products and to assess its long-term effectiveness and safety.

Obstacles can derail vaccine development at any step in the process. For instance, a vaccine might be shelved due to a lack of funding for research. Or it could be stopped because of safety concerns, lack of effectiveness, or lack of public or political interest. Or pharmaceutical companies may not be interested in producing it if it's expensive to manufacture or they fear losing money on it.

Often vaccine development depends on who is worried about a particular disease. For instance, the Public Health Agency of Canada oversaw the creation of a vaccine for the Ebola virus. But the vaccine sat on the shelf for more than a decade without much interest after its development in 2005. After the biggest Ebola epidemic in history hit West Africa in 2014 and the virus infected two US nurses, interest in the vaccine spiked, and making an effective Ebola vaccine available suddenly became a top priority. Within two years, a clinical trial led to a promising vaccine that's several steps closer to becoming a reality. As the Ebola vaccine's story shows, social acceptance is essential for vaccine development: Is the disease frightening enough or causing enough death and disability to justify a vaccine? Do enough people care about stopping the disease? Are enough people willing to get the vaccine? Will the public tolerate the vaccine's possible side effects? A "no" to any of these could derail a vaccine's development. Only a fraction of the hundreds of vaccines scientists try to develop ever pass regulatory requirements.

MAURICE HILLEMAN, VACCINE DEVELOPER EXTRAORDINAIRE

Unlike the Ebola vaccine, the polio vaccine had immense public support behind it from the start. Then, shortly after its development in 1955, the world entered a golden age of vaccine development. From the 1960s to the 1980s, scientists developed vaccines for measles, mumps, rubella, meningitis, pneumonia, yellow fever, hepatitis B, typhoid, and Hib. Teams across the world contributed to the effort. One man, Maurice Hilleman, became "the premier vaccinologist of the twentieth century," says Paul Offit, codeveloper of the rotavirus vaccine and head of the Division of Infectious Disease at Children's Hospital of Philadelphia in Pennsylvania.

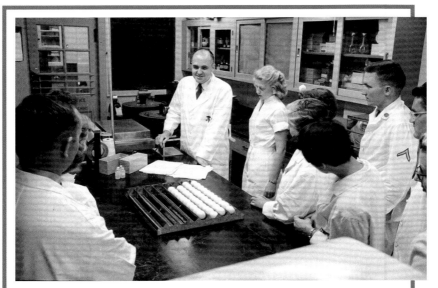

Maurice Hilleman talks with his scientific team at the Walter Reed Army Institute of Research in Silver Spring, Maryland, in 1957. A tray full of chicken eggs sits on the center of the table. Vaccinologists use egg whites to grow the viruses and bacteria for making vaccines.

Hilleman developed more than forty vaccines, including those for hepatitis A and hepatitis B, chickenpox, measles, mumps, rubella, meningitis, pneumonia, and Hib. He also discovered hepatitis A and other viruses. According to Anthony Fauci, director of the US National Institute of Allergy and Infectious Diseases, "If you look at the whole field of vaccinology, nobody was more influential."

Hilleman was born in Montana in August 1919. He studied microbiology and chemistry at the University of Chicago. At the age of twenty-five, while working at the pharmaceutical company E. R. Squibb & Sons in New Brunswick, New Jersey, Hilleman developed his first vaccine, against Japanese encephalitis. Hilleman "was a ridiculously driven, hard-working man, phenomenally logical and really tough and hard-nosed," said Offit. "He was this combination of brilliance and toughness. He expected everyone to be as driven as him."

At one in the morning on March 21, 1963, Hilleman's five-year-old daughter, Jeryl Lynn, developed a sore throat, fever, and swollen glands. Hilleman recognized the symptoms of mumps, a disease that in some cases led to deafness. By then Hilleman was working for another pharmaceutical company, Merck. He drove to his laboratory to get the equipment to swab, or scrape cells from, the inside of Jeryl Lynn's mouth. Then he returned to the lab to store the cells in a freezer. Hilleman used that sample to isolate the mumps virus from Jeryl Lynn's cells and to grow more of the virus in his laboratory so he could study it. By the end of 1967, he had developed a mumps vaccine. His other daughter, Kirsten, was among the first children to be vaccinated in trials of the vaccine.

Over the next two decades, Hilleman developed more vaccines than any other scientist in history, including eight of the fourteen vaccines recommended for children by the CDC. The last vaccine Hilleman created, against hepatitis B, was licensed in 1981. It was the first vaccine developed using human blood and the first vaccine to prevent a type of cancer (liver cancer). "His work was unprecedented, and he will remain forever unmatched as the most prolific vaccine developer in history," Offit said. "He did everything for the right reasons. It was never about him. It was always about doing something to help children to keep them from dying."

THE SHIFTY, DRIFTY FLU VIRUS

All organisms evolve from one generation to the next. Mutations, or sudden changes in genes, occur randomly in each new generation. If a certain mutation improves an organism's chances of survival, the organism will thrive and reproduce. Often its offspring also have the genetic mutation. In this way, the change gradually becomes a permanent part of that species' genetic makeup. For example, some species of mice and bedbugs have evolved to survive the poisons and pesticides humans use to try to kill them. Through evolution,

The flu virus can jump from birds and other animals to humans. To keep flu from spreading through both animal and human populations, workers sometimes vaccinate farm animals. Here, Chinese health workers vaccinate chickens at a poultry farm.

dogs (unlike their wolf ancestors) developed the ability to bark to communicate with humans.

Microbes also evolve. When they reproduce, random mutations in their genetic material are passed on to their offspring. This process can take thousands or millions of years in complex organisms such as reptiles or mammals. But in single-celled microbes, it can happen in months or minutes. Some viruses, such as measles, are stable and mutate little over time. Others, such as influenza, mutate so rapidly that vaccinologists can barely keep up. Because the flu virus changes so quickly, vaccinologists must develop a new flu vaccine each year.

The flu virus mutates rapidly for two reasons. First, its genetic material is made of ribonucleic acid (RNA) instead of DNA. RNA, like DNA, is a collection of molecules that carry instructions for how the organism will grow and function. RNA has only one strand of genes, whereas DNA has two. When DNA replicates, the cell double-checks one strand against the other to be sure genes are copied correctly. RNA doesn't have this double-checking feature, so mutations get missed. The flu virus also replicates very quickly, and its rapid replication speed leads to many genetic mistakes.

The influenza virus undergoes two different types of mutations. In antigenic drift, the virus's genetic material changes slightly, resulting in a new strain of the virus. The new strain is different enough from the old strain that researchers must develop a new vaccine to combat it.

Antigenic shift is more dramatic—and more dangerous. The flu virus comes in three types—A, B, and C. Types B and C infect only humans. Type A is a zoonotic disease: it infects humans as well as several other animals, including pigs many kinds of birds, dogs, and horses. It can jump from one species to another. This jumping makes type A flu virus more susceptible to major genetic mutations. After an influenza A virus jumps from a nonhuman species to a human, it can rapidly undergo changes in the human's cells. The result is an entirely new subtype of the virus. In another scenario, if two A strains of flu infect one organism at the same time, the genetic material can combine in the cells, creating a new subtype of flu virus. Most people will have no preexisting immunity to the brand-new subtype, so almost everyone who encounters the virus will get sick. The result could be a flu pandemic, or a worldwide epidemic of the disease. The most famous flu pandemic occurred in 1918 and 1919, when Spanish influenza infected one-fifth of the world's population. That pandemic was the result of antigenic shift, and humans had never encountered that strain or anything similar to it before. It was not until the late 1990s that scientists had the technology to identify that flu strain's RNA and to determine that it likely came from a bird flu strain. The disease killed more than half a million Americans and killed twenty to fifty million people worldwide.

Maurice Hilleman was the scientist who figured out how antigenic drift and shift work. This discovery helped him recognize the influenza strain of 1957 as new and dangerous, created through antigenic shift. He created a vaccine that pharmaceutical companies mass-produced in just four months. Although seventy thousand Americans died of flu during the 1957–1958 flu season, experts estimate that one million would have died if not for Hilleman's vaccine.

When the H1N1 strain of flu appeared in late 2009, experts worried because it was a new subtype. Worse, it greatly resembled the H1N1 subtype that had caused the 1918–1919 Spanish flu pandemic. Pharmaceutical companies rushed out a new vaccine that year, but the flu strain still hit young and middle-aged adults hard, just as it had in the Spanish pandemic. Elderly adults fared better. Why? Epidemiologists think that elderly adults—born in the early and middle twentieth century—might have been exposed years earlier to variations of the 1918 flu subtype. This exposure may have given them some immunity to the similar 2009 strain.

THE VACCINE THAT WASN'T

The story of the Lyme disease vaccine shows how poor timing and misinformation can derail a safe, effective vaccine. Lyme disease is caused by the *Borrelia burgdorferi* bacteria, which is carried by tiny animals called deer ticks. If a deer tick bites a human, it can release the bacteria into the person's bloodstream. Lyme disease often starts with a bull's-eye-shaped rash, and symptoms progress to fever, headaches, and fatigue. Approximately three hundred thousand Americans and sixty-five thousand to eighty-five thousand Europeans contract Lyme disease every year.

A simple antibiotic easily cures Lyme disease. But doctors often misdiagnose the illness because Lyme symptoms resemble those of other illnesses, and many people never develop the telltale rash. In addition, many people do not notice or recall being bitten by a tick. Without treatment, Lyme disease can cause facial paralysis, shooting muscle pains, arthritis, and speech and memory problems. Severe infections can cause meningitis, heart problems, nervous system disorders, and sometimes death.

In 1998 the FDA approved the LYMErix vaccine, which was 76 percent effective. It worked differently than other vaccines. It did not create antibodies in the vaccinated person. Instead, if a vaccinated person was bitten by an infected deer tick, the vaccine traveled into the tick's gut while the tick was biting and feeding on the person's blood. In other words, the vaccine killed *B. burgdorferi* inside the tick before it reached the person's bloodstream.

However, several problems caused the vaccine's downfall. A person needed to receive three doses—a second dose a month after the first and a third dose twelve months later—to receive full protection. Needing multiple doses spread across a year made it more difficult for people to get the complete series of immunizations. Children ages two to fifteen have the highest risk of Lyme disease infection, but the FDA approved the vaccine only for those over seventeen because the pharmaceutical company that developed it had not conducted clinical trials in children early enough to submit that data to the FDA. Later trials showed the vaccine to be safe and effective in children. However, approval of the vaccine for children required a new application to the FDA. Because each application costs millions of dollars, the pharmaceutical company did not pursue it. Also, only approximately twenty thousand to thirty thousand cases of the disease were reported each year, but estimated infections were actually three to five times higher. The age restriction and underreporting of the disease led the CDC to issue only a weak recommendation for the vaccine. As a result, the American public had little confidence in it.

In addition, some critics claimed that the vaccine caused serious side effects, including arthritis and damage to the immune system. Evidence did not support these claims, and later studies showed no such risks. Still, in late 1999, a group sued the drug company, claiming that the vaccine had harmed more than one hundred recipients. Because of the bad publicity and weak CDC recommendation, sales of the vaccine dropped from $40 million in 1999 to $5 million in 2001. The drug company permanently withdrew the vaccine the next year.

More than fifteen years later, vaccinologists have yet to develop another vaccine for humans for Lyme disease. Stanley Plotkin calls the loss of the Lyme vaccine "the worst recent failure to use an effective vaccine."

DILEMMA OF THE PERTUSSIS VACCINE

In the early twentieth century, pertussis was a major cause of death and disability among children. Throughout the 1920s, pertussis killed about six thousand children every year in the United States, more than diphtheria, scarlet fever, or measles. Pertussis peaked in 1934 with more than 260,000 US cases.

After Pearl Kendrick and Grace Eldering of the Michigan Department of Health developed a vaccine for pertussis in the late 1930s, cases dropped by 99 percent. In 1948 vaccinologists combined the diphtheria, tetanus, and pertussis vaccines into one shot called DTP.

The DTP vaccine was not without side effects. It sometimes caused reactions, including fevers that could cause seizures. The seizures did not cause long-term damage, but they were frightening. In the 1980s, concerns about DTP's safety led to the development of new pertussis-containing vaccines that were less likely to cause reactions. The DTP vaccine contained whole pertussis bacteria cells. The new vaccines, called DTaP and Tdap, contained only two or three proteins from the pertussis bacteria. This type of vaccine is called an acellular vaccine because it does not contain whole cells (the prefix *a* means "without"). The tetanus and diphtheria portions of the vaccines did not change.

THE WOMEN BEHIND THE PERTUSSIS VACCINE

Scientists learned in 1906 that the *Bordetella pertussis* bacteria caused whooping cough, but attempts to create vaccines throughout the 1920s all failed. Then, in 1932, a severe pertussis outbreak hit Grand Rapids, Michigan. That same year, the Michigan Department of Health laboratory director had hired bacteriologists Pearl Kendrick and Grace Eldering. He specifically recruited women because he had a limited budget and could pay women lower salaries than men. Kendrick and Eldering collected samples of fresh pertussis bacteria from infected children. The two developed a way to grow the bacteria quickly in the lab and learned that pertussis is contagious for four to five weeks. Kendrick asked the director for permission to develop a general pertussis vaccine. Somewhat dismissively he told her, "Go ahead and do all you can with pertussis if it amuses you."

Kendrick (*top*) and Eldering (*bottom*)

Kendrick and Eldering used the lab after hours and raised donations to fund their work. They inactivated the bacteria with thimerosal. They tested an experimental vaccine on themselves and local families. In 1934 and 1935, the two women conducted a large controlled trial of a pertussis vaccine, with 712 vaccinated and 880 unvaccinated children. Only 4 vaccinated children developed mild pertussis; 45 unvaccinated children in the community came down with serious pertussis. The results showed that the vaccine was 89 percent effective.

By 1940 children across the United States were receiving Kendrick and Eldering's vaccine. The number of pertussis cases dropped by 76 percent between 1934 and 1948. By 1960 cases had dropped by 95 percent.

However, the number of pertussis cases reported to public health agencies began to rise, first very gradually in the 1980s and then more dramatically in the 1990s. One reason for the higher reported numbers was that pediatricians and family doctors were becoming better at recognizing pertussis. They were testing more children and adults for the disease. So doctors reported cases that might have gone undiagnosed earlier. But cases were rising in infants too.

Epidemiologists suspected that the immunity provided by the DTaP and Tdap vaccines was waning earlier than expected. A study in 2012 confirmed that suspicion. Further studies of DTaP and Tdap showed even more clearly that acellular vaccines are not as effective over time as are whole-cell vaccines. Some studies showed effectiveness dropping by almost half in two or three years.

In 2013 scientists at the FDA found another possible contributor to increasing pertussis rates. Experiments showed that baboons vaccinated with acellular pertussis vaccines could still carry the disease and transmit it to others—even if they didn't show symptoms. This phenomenon is called asymptomatic carriage. The immune systems of baboons and humans are similar, so asymptomatic carriage likely happens in humans too. The study suggested that acellular pertussis vaccines probably don't maintain much herd immunity, since vaccination doesn't stop transmission of the bacteria. Similarly, cocooning (vaccinating other household members to protect an unvaccinated newborn) probably isn't effective either. So the CDC recommends that all pregnant women get the Tdap vaccine in their last trimester (third of three periods of pregnancy), so that the fetus receives antibodies made by the mother. Research since then has shown that maternal antibodies from vaccination during pregnancy are up to 90 percent effective in preventing pertussis in newborns. Finally, new evidence in the same period suggested that some pertussis bacteria strains had mutated slightly in response to the vaccine. The vaccine still works but may be slightly less effective against the mutated

PASSIVE IMMUNITY

Having antibodies against a disease without getting sick from or receiving a vaccine for that disease is called passive immunity. A person can gain passive immunity in two ways. An injection of antibodies, called immunoglobulin, taken from other people or manufactured in a lab, can give someone temporary passive immunity in some emergency situations. During pregnancy, any antibodies the mother developed from past infections or vaccines are transferred to the fetus. The fetus then has passive immunity against those diseases for several months after birth.

Giving mothers the pertussis vaccine during pregnancy protects newborns against the disease for much of their first year of life. Passive immunity also influences vaccine recommendations. For instance, mothers' measles antibodies last about a year in babies, so babies don't receive the measles vaccine until they turn one.

strains. Scientists aren't sure because they don't fully understand the relationship between the pertussis antigens and the immune system's response. Several research teams are working on developing new pertussis vaccines, but the process is slow and expensive. No one knows when vaccinologists will have a more effective vaccine.

THE STORY OF ROTASHIELD

The story of the first rotavirus vaccine demonstrates the effectiveness of the US vaccine safety system. More than half a million children under the age of five die from rotavirus every year—that's about fourteen hundred children every day.

Before a vaccine was available, rotavirus affected 2.7 million children and caused fifty-five thousand to seventy thousand hospitalizations in the United States each year. Most US children with rotavirus survived due to the high quality of medical care in the United States, but the disease killed 500,000 children around the world. The approval of the RotaShield vaccine in August 1998 was great news—at first.

Soon after the vaccine's approval, fifteen infants in the United States developed a bowel obstruction called intussusception after getting RotaShield. Nine of these infants needed surgery.

The CDC temporarily suspended its recommendation for the vaccine and conducted two emergency studies. The research found that healthy children under the age of one were twenty to thirty times more likely to get intussusception within two weeks of receiving the first dose of RotaShield than those who did not get the vaccine. After a second dose of RotaShield, the risk of intussusception was three to seven times greater. Researchers concluded that one in every ten thousand doses of RotaShield would cause intussusception. So about a year after the vaccine was licensed, the CDC permanently removed its recommendation for RotaShield. The manufacturer voluntarily pulled RotaShield from distribution.

How did a vaccine that caused intussusception get approved in the first place? During trials, 10,054 infants received RotaShield, and 5 of them got intussusception. But in the control group (test subjects who receive no treatment so they can be compared to those who do), of 4,633 infants who didn't get the vaccine, one case of intussusception occurred. These percentages (0.05 and 0.022) were similar enough that they didn't seem to show that the vaccine was causing intussusception. Further, one case of intussusception occurs normally among every two to three thousand children in the general population. For this reason, intussusception rates during the trials looked like the normal expected rates in a typical population.

However, the clinical trials did not include enough children to detect very rare side effects. With only ten thousand children receiving the vaccine in the trials, the cases of intussusception looked like chance occurrences. Meanwhile, two more rotavirus vaccines, Rotarix and RotaTeq, were in development. The trials for these vaccines each included about sixty thousand children. That was enough to ensure that even very rare side effects would show up in some of the tested children.

The FDA approved Rotarix and RotaTeq, which protect about 98 percent of the children who receive either vaccine from rotavirus disease. Research suggests that these vaccines may carry a tiny risk of intussusception—in about one of every one hundred thousand children vaccinated. But that risk is outweighed by the greater risk of one in every sixty-five unvaccinated children being hospitalized with rotavirus. Additionally, in rare cases, rotavirus itself can cause intussusception. So the risks of the new vaccines are more acceptable than those of RotaShield.

A MISUNDERSTOOD VACCINE

HPV is the most common sexually transmitted disease (STD) anywhere. More than 90 percent of men and 80 percent of women will have an HPV infection at some point in their lives, yet most will never know it. A handful of HPV strains cause genital warts, but most strains cause no symptoms or harm. The immune system defeats the infection on its own. However, of the more than 150 strains of HPV, 13 can cause several types of cancer.

Cervical cancer is almost always caused by HPV and is a leading cause of death for women in poor nations, who usually don't get regular cervical cancer screenings. Even in the United States, where most women receive routine screening, more than four thousand women die from the disease each year. HPV also causes 95 percent of anal cancers, 65 percent of vaginal cancers, 50 percent of vulvar cancers, 35 percent of penile cancers, and 70 percent of throat cancers.

Researchers trying to develop an HPV vaccine kept failing— until scientists at the NIH discovered they needed to rearrange the configuration of proteins in the vaccine. After that breakthrough, in 1992, the vaccine worked "like gangbusters," said one of its developers, John Schiller.

But Schiller's team couldn't find a drug company willing to

Some parents object to HPV vaccination for young teens because they believe it encourages teen sex, but many studies prove it does not. Research shows that the vaccine saves lives by protecting young people from HPV-caused cancers.

manufacture the vaccine. The companies all noted that many earlier vaccines against STDs had failed. They feared that Schiller's HPV vaccine would fail too. Maurice Hilleman at Merck was the exception. "Where others saw problems, Dr. Hilleman saw opportunities," Schiller said. Merck produced the first HPV vaccine, Gardasil, in 2006. It produced another vaccine to protect against more strains of HPV in 2015. These two HPV vaccines protect against 90 percent of all HPV-caused cancers.

The HPV vaccine should have been an immediate and stunning success. But that's not what happened. The CDC recommended girls receive the vaccine between ages eleven and thirteen. The CDC targeted this age range because HPV vaccine is most effective in people who have not yet encountered the virus. Girls aged eleven to thirteen are less likely to be sexually active and thus less likely to get HVP than are older girls. In addition, the vaccine creates a stronger antibody response in younger girls than in older adolescents. For this reason, adolescents under the age of fifteen need only two doses while those fifteen and older need three. The CDC initially only recommended the vaccine for girls, but it expanded the recommendation to include boys in 2011.

But some parents worried that getting a vaccine against an STD would encourage their children to think sex was safe and to therefore engage in sexual activity. Studies showed this was not the case, but some parents still saw the CDC as supporting teen sex. For their part, CDC officials viewed the vaccine as a way to save lives.

Uneasiness about teen sex then shifted toward anxiety about dangerous side effects. Some feared the HPV vaccine caused blood clots and other health problems. Researchers investigated and found no evidence for the claims. More studies have established that the HPV vaccine is one of the safest vaccines the CDC recommends. HPV vaccination rates have been improving, but because of the vaccine's rocky start, rates remain far below those of other routine vaccines. It is a vaccine that can prevent almost 5 percent of all cancers worldwide, yet millions are still unprotected.

04

PUSHBACK AGAINST VACCINES

Even before Edward Jenner introduced the world to vaccination, many were skeptical. The idea seemed nonsensical. How could exposing a person to a disease prevent that same disease? In Jenner's day, no one understood how the immune system worked, so it's understandable that some resisted vaccination. In addition, vaccination and variolation weren't always safe in earlier centuries. Transferring infected material directly from one person's arm to another's, either through physical contact or using nonsterile instruments, could transmit syphilis, hepatitis, and other diseases. And in some cases, people developed full-blown smallpox after variolation or vaccination. Even without a full-blown infection, recently variolated people could still transmit the disease to others they encountered. In addition, some people distrusted scientists and government. For these reasons, the anti-vaccination movement took hold at the turn of the nineteenth century, emerging alongside the first vaccine. Anti-vaccinationists claimed, for example, that Jenner's smallpox vaccine could cause severe side effects, such as turning humans into cows or making cow parts grow from human bodies, although scientific evidence did not support such far-fetched claims. Other people believed that it was unholy and unclean to infect someone with material that had originally come from a diseased cow.

Britain passed the first mandatory vaccination laws in the mid-nineteenth century. These laws made smallpox vaccination free for

Opposition to vaccination has existed for centuries. In this British cartoon from 1802, vaccinated patients are shown with cow heads and other cow parts growing from their bodies. The cartoon reflects public doubts about vaccine safety at the time.

the poor and required vaccination for everyone under the age of fourteen. The laws also banned variolation since it is riskier than vaccination. Parents who refused to have their children vaccinated could be fined or imprisoned. Anti-vaccinationists pushed back, forming organizations and publishing journals such as the *Anti-Vaccinator* and the *Vaccination Inquirer.*

Anti-vaccinationists argued that vaccines were ineffective and could be deadly—both of which were true, but only in rare cases. They claimed that 80 percent of smallpox victims had actually been vaccinated and that vaccination killed twenty-five thousand British children a year. After more than one hundred thousand citizens in the British city of Leicester protested against the laws in 1885, the British government eased its vaccination requirements. The Vaccination Act of 1898 allowed parents to refuse vaccination for their children and removed penalties for those who did not vaccinate.

The anti-vaccination movement soon spread to the United States. Anti-vaccination leagues formed in New England and New York. US anti-vaccinators successfully fought state laws requiring vaccination in California, Illinois, Indiana, Minnesota, Utah, West Virginia, and Wisconsin. In Boston, Massachusetts, Pastor Henning Jacobson challenged a law requiring residents to be vaccinated during smallpox outbreaks. Jacobson argued that forced vaccination was "hostile to the inherent right of every freeman to care for his own body and health in such way as to him seems best" and was "nothing short of an assault upon his person." The case went all the way to the US Supreme Court, which in 1905 ruled against Jacobson. The court said that mandatory vaccination was legal because individuals' rights cannot override the public's right to protect itself from dangerous contagious diseases.

At the same time, there was some truth to the fears about vaccinations. For instance, in 1901, nine children in Camden, New Jersey, died from smallpox vaccines that had somehow been contaminated with tetanus. The same year, thirteen children in Saint Louis, Missouri, died from a diphtheria antitoxin contaminated with tetanus because the animal (a horse) used to produce the antitoxin was also infected with tetanus. (An antitoxin is an injection of antibodies, created by another organism's immune system, that treats an infection caused by a bacterial toxin.) To make vaccines safer, the US government passed the Biologics Control Act of 1902. This law set forth safety regulations that manufacturers had to follow when producing vaccines.

VACCINE REFUSAL IN THE TWENTIETH CENTURY

Fast-forward to the late 1970s, by which point vaccines for polio, tetanus, diphtheria, pertussis, measles, mumps, and rubella had all been developed. By this time, all fifty states required a set of vaccinations for children before they could attend their first year of school. Vaccines were an accepted fact of life in the United States.

That changed on April 18, 1982, when NBC aired a one-hour television documentary called *DPT: Vaccine Roulette*. The program described the supposed risks of the DPT vaccine, which were said to include seizures, brain damage, uncontrollable screaming, and nonresponsiveness in children. The show featured interviews with scientists, lawyers, policy makers, and angry parents; stories of children allegedly harmed by the vaccine; and photographs of dead babies allegedly killed by vaccines. The documentary claimed that the US government, doctors, and the pharmaceutical industry had covered up the risks and that the vaccine was not effective in preventing pertussis. The show won an Emmy Award for excellence in television programming even though it had employed several elements of irresponsible journalism. The filmmakers never verified the parents' stories about their children's conditions with medical evidence and never provided evidence showing that the vaccine had caused the damage.

COGNITIVE BIASES

Those who fear or oppose vaccination often do so because of cognitive biases, or ways of thinking that can lead to illogical conclusions. People come to illogical, false conclusions about many things and for many reasons. A set of cognitive biases, or ways of thinking that strongly favor one thing over another, can lead to such conclusions. Psychologists recognize several types of cognitive biases:

- **Omission bias** is the perception that doing nothing is less harmful than taking action. This bias can lead people to think that vaccinating carries more risk than not vaccinating. No approved vaccine is 100 percent safe. But scientific research proves that the risks of vaccines are far lower than the risks of disease. Benjamin Franklin, famous American scientist, statesman, and inventor, learned the hard way how omission bias can lead to poor choices. He wrote, "In 1736 I lost one of my sons, a fine boy of four years old, by the smallpox taken in the common way. I long regretted bitterly and still regret that I had not given it to him by inoculation. This I mention for the sake of the parents who omit that operation, on the supposition that they should never forgive themselves if a child died under it; my example showing that the regret may be the same either way, and that, therefore, the safer [inoculation] should be chosen." At first, omission bias had led Franklin to believe that not inoculating his son was the safest choice—a decision he came to regret.w

- **Availability bias** is when a person focuses on a recent, dramatic, and often rare event rather than on a larger, more common risk. For example, someone who hears about a recent shark attack might fear sharks more than drowning at the beach, even though drowning is much more likely. Similarly, parents who hear about the harm of a vaccine, whether or not it's true, might focus on this story rather than on the danger of measles or another preventable disease.

- **Negativity bias** involves the brain focusing more on negative information than positive information. So if you receive ten compliments and one insult in a day, you're likely to remember the insult more than the compliments. This bias can lead people to focus on the slight risks of vaccines rather than their benefits.
- **Confirmation bias** involves unconsciously preferring information that confirms what you already believe. Anyone searching for information on vaccines online will find pro- and anti-vaccine websites. But those who already believe that vaccines are unsafe will be more likely to read and pay attention to the anti-vaccine sites. Confirmation bias can be so powerful that confronting people with proof that they are wrong can backfire and strengthen their erroneous belief.
- **In-group bias** occurs when people with the same opinions share and reinforce their beliefs. People tend to trust members of their own social group more than outsiders, whom they might fear or dislike. So those who believe that vaccines are dangerous often stick together, reinforce their belief by sharing them with one another, and dismiss the ideas of those who say that vaccines are safe.

In addition to these biases, the human brain is not wired to assess risk very well. Correctly estimating risk involves complex calculations based on limited information. Emotions and experiences shape how people process that information. For example, many people desperately fear flying but not driving—even though a car crash is statistically much more likely than a plane crash. But giving people accurate information about the risks doesn't necessarily change their minds. Driving still *feels* safer because it's more familiar. Cognitive biases can interfere with attempts to evaluate risk even when people believe they are thinking rationally.

Additionally, they manipulated interviews with doctors to make it appear, falsely, that the medical professionals felt the vaccine was to blame.

"Doctors were blindsided, and parents were up in arms," said Paul Offit about *Vaccine Roulette*. "The program gave birth to anti-vaccine groups and a congressional hearing to determine whether vaccines were doing more harm than good." Twenty-five years later, researchers found that many of the children in the documentary had suffered from Dravet syndrome, a genetic disorder that has nothing to do with vaccines.

Factual or not, that single hour of television launched a movement against vaccines that completely reshaped the way Americans thought about immunization. One group of concerned parents formed Dissatisfied Parents Together (DPT) to advocate for improved vaccine safety, better information on vaccine risks, and parents' rights to decide whether or not to vaccinate their children.

Meanwhile, hundreds of parents filed lawsuits against vaccine manufacturers such as Wyeth Laboratories and Lederle. The parents wanted compensation for brain damage and other injuries they claimed the DTP vaccine had caused in their children. Vaccines had never been highly profitable for pharmaceutical companies. With the threat of costly, high-profile lawsuits, many drug companies decided to stop making vaccines altogether. This worried public health officials because vaccine shortages could result if too many pharmaceutical companies stopped making vaccines.

Facing lawsuits, Wyeth Laboratories and Lederle stopped making DTP, saying that lawsuit costs were two hundred times greater than DTP sales. Lederle eventually began making the DTP vaccine again but increased the price from seventeen cents per dose to eleven dollars per dose to pay for legal costs.

As the lawsuits piled up, a new leader emerged from the DTP parent group. Barbara Loe Fisher, a thirty-four-year-old publicist in Alexandria,

Barbara Loe Fisher gave momentum to the anti-vaccination movement when she organized the National Vaccine Information Center in 1991. Here she speaks against a California vaccination bill introduced by Dr. Richard Pan (*standing*).

Virginia, claimed that her four-year-old son, Christian, had been harmed by the DTP vaccine. She said that after receiving his third dose, he stared into space for hours, not responding normally to his mother. Fisher became a driving force in the overhaul of vaccine safety laws in the United States. She served on several vaccine safety committees at the HHS, the Institute of Medicine (a private medical organization, later renamed the National Academy of Medicine), and the FDA.

NEW SYSTEMS AND LAWS

Parent activists such as Barbara Loe Fisher pushed concerns about vaccine safety into the national spotlight. Then came increasing lawsuits against pharmaceutical companies and the public health community's worries about vaccine shortages and returning diseases. Together, these factors led to the National Childhood Vaccine Injury Act, signed by President Ronald Reagan on November 14, 1986.

The law created the National Vaccine Injury Compensation Program. Through this program, parents who believe that their children have been harmed by vaccines can receive money to pay for a child's lifetime medical care, or $250,000 if the child has died. To receive the money, the child must have an injury listed in government documents as possibly caused by vaccines or else the parents must provide a "preponderance of evidence" supporting their claim. That is, they must show that there's more than a 50 percent chance that their story of vaccine injury is true. Many top CDC and FDA scientists have opposed the program because they see compensation being made without sufficient scientific evidence. In addition, parents make their cases before judges who do not usually have scientific or medical training. Of more than seventeen thousand claims filed since the program began, about five thousand have been compensated. Many of these cases involved injuries, health problems, or deaths that research shows almost certainly were not caused by vaccines. However, the federal government designed the program to favor parents, even with weak evidence that an injury might be linked to a vaccine.

The 1986 law created the National Vaccine Program Office. To better educate parents, the office requires health-care providers across the country to give all parents standardized Vaccine Information Statements (VISs) before their children receive recommended vaccines. Each VIS explains a particular vaccine's purpose, the symptoms of the diseases the vaccine prevents, and who should or shouldn't get the vaccine. The VIS also explains the research-based risks of the vaccine and what to do if a serious reaction occurs.

The 1986 law also set up the Vaccine Adverse Event Reporting System (VAERS). Parents, health-care providers, and vaccine recipients can report any health problems occurring after vaccination to this system. The data collected in VAERS is very helpful to scientists looking for unknown side effects of vaccines. If multiple people report the same problem about the same vaccine, and if there is a biological reason the vaccine could have caused the problem, scientists can design studies to see whether the vaccine and the problem are related. This is how scientists found the link between intussusception and the first rotavirus vaccine. However, not everything reported to VAERS is caused by a vaccine. For instance, one VAERS record noted that a "patient accidentally fell in open well (granite quarry filled with water), drowned and expired . . . 49 days [after] receiving first dose of Gardasil," an HPV vaccine. Over the years, anti-vaccination groups have quoted stories in VAERS as evidence that vaccines cause all kinds of health problems. In reality, only large, well-designed studies can determine whether a vaccine causes a particular reaction.

Barbara Loe Fisher didn't feel that the 1986 law went far enough. She believed that parents should have complete control over whether or not to vaccinate their children and that schools should not require immunizations. So she transformed the DPT group into the National Vaccine Information Center (NVIC) in 1991. The group has become the largest, most influential anti-vaccine organization in the United States. It claims to be pro-vaccine safety and not anti-vaccine. Critics of the group point out, however, that it spread misinformation about vaccines and rejects much solid research showing the safety of vaccines.

Around this time, during the first half of 1989, cases of measles in the United States suddenly shot up five times higher than usual. Most of those who came down with measles had not been vaccinated. Over the next two years, more than fifty-five thousand US measles cases resulted in eleven thousand hospitalizations and 123 deaths, especially among infants too young to be vaccinated. Public health officials determined that the epidemic was caused by large numbers of children not receiving the recommended measles vaccination at the age of twelve to fifteen months. Some parents deliberately skipped the vaccine, some couldn't afford it, and others were unable to bring their children to a clinic. In addition, some clinics did not have enough staff or supplies to meet public demand. The epidemic also sickened many young adults who received the single recommended dose of measles vaccine as children but whose immune systems did not respond strongly to the single dose. The CDC therefore began recommending two doses of the measles vaccine, which is 98 to 99 percent effective.

The outbreak led public health authorities to review procedures to prevent future epidemics. It led to a new federal program called Vaccines for Children. Created in 1993, the program pays for vaccinations for children under the age of nineteen whose families lack health insurance or who can't afford vaccines. The program has greatly improved measles vaccination coverage across the United States. Coverage rose to 90 percent for children under three by 1996, compared to less than 70 percent before 1990. In 2000 officials announced that measles had been eliminated from the United States.

THE WAKEFIELD SCANDAL

Andrew Wakefield was a British gastroenterologist—a doctor who treats problems of the digestive system. On February 28, 1998, he gave a press conference at the Royal Free Hospital School of Medicine in London, England. He and twelve coauthors had just published a study about twelve children in the *Lancet*, one of Britain's oldest and most prestigious medical journals. The children had supposedly been developing normally and then suddenly lost language and other mental abilities. Nine of them had been diagnosed with autism, a disability marked by difficulties in communication and interactions with others. They also developed diarrhea and stomach pain. According to Wakefield, the parents stated that these changes had occurred after the children had received the MMR vaccine. Later investigation showed, however, that Wakefield had changed and falsified the children's medical information in the study. Some of the children had shown symptoms of autism before vaccination. Others did not have autism at all or began developing normally later. In most of the children, normal constipation had caused the stomach pain. But at the press conference, Wakefield said he believed that the MMR vaccine had caused the autism and a new intestinal disorder together.

However, the study itself did not suggest that the MMR vaccine caused autism. It stated only that the autism symptoms and the vaccination had occurred around the same time. This kind of observational study cannot show that one thing caused another. Only a study comparing two randomly divided groups of children can show causation. In addition, a group of twelve children is too small for a study to come to any firm conclusions. Even so, Wakefield publicly stated—on his own— that to prevent risk of autism, children should receive only a single measles vaccine instead of the full MMR. The event immediately made headlines throughout Britain. Autism was not new. But because autism diagnoses were rising, the condition was in the headlines. Many parents were desperate to avoid anything that might "cause autism" in their children, so MMR vaccination rates in Britain began dropping. Just five years after the press conference, vaccination rates had dropped from 91 percent to 80 percent.

Andrew Wakefield, a prominent gastroenterologist in Britain, published a small study about a possible link between autism and the MMR vaccine. Journalist Brian Deer exposed the study as fraudulent, but by then, a new anti-vaccine movement focusing on autism fears had begun.

CONFUSING CORRELATION AND CAUSATION

One job of the brain is to make sense of the world, so it looks for patterns such as cause and effect. If one thing happens after another, such as getting sick soon after a flu shot, the brain might connect the two events. The person might mistakenly think the vaccine caused the illness, when in fact it did not. Two things happening around the same time is known as correlation. One thing causing the other is referred to as causation. Scientists and other experts caution the public not to confuse correlation with causation.

This confusion contributes to fears about vaccines and autism. Babies typically start using words between twelve and eighteen months and begin pointing to objects by eighteen months. But babies of this age with autism may not speak, make eye contact, or point. Babies receive the MMR and other vaccines between twelve and fifteen months—about the same time the first symptoms appear in autistic children. Some parents then confuse correlation with causation and mistakenly believe that the vaccines caused their child's autism.

To learn whether one thing does cause another, scientists design studies that compare two groups of people. One group is exposed to the suspected cause; the other is not. If the supposed effect occurs more often in the exposed group, then the exposure probably did cause the effect. If rates of the effect are about the same in both groups, the exposure is not the culprit. Scientists showed that vaccines do not cause autism by showing that rates of autism were about the same in groups that had and had not received the MMR or other vaccines at the time of each study.

Across the ocean in the United States, autism diagnoses were also rising. As in Britain, some American parents believed that vaccines cause autism. But they had not heard about Andrew Wakefield's claims about the MMR vaccine yet. Instead, their fears focused on one particular vaccine ingredient—thimerosal.

Thimerosal is a mercury-based preservative used in several childhood vaccines to prevent bacterial or fungal contamination. Some types of mercury, such as the methylmercury found in some fish, are neurotoxins. They build up in the body and can harm the brain if a person consumes too much. But the type of mercury in thimerosal, ethylmercury, exits the body within a week or two of being taken in. No research has shown that ethylmercury harms the body. Still, some scientists argued that more research was needed to be certain that the tiny amount of thimerosal in vaccines wasn't causing brain damage.

In 1999 the FDA recommended removing thimerosal from vaccines—just to be on the safe side. The recommendation itself was controversial. Some vaccine experts worried that it suggested that thimerosal was unsafe, despite lack of evidence showing so. Would the recommendation reduce parents' confidence in vaccine safety?

Based on the FDA recommendation, manufacturers removed thimerosal from all vaccines recommended for children under six, except for the flu vaccine. Researchers continued studying the preservative. After reviewing more than two hundred studies, the Institute of Medicine concluded in 2004 that research "consistently provided evidence of no association between thimerosal-containing vaccines and autism."

But as many people had anticipated, removing thimerosal aroused suspicion among many parents. Some asked, if thimerosal wasn't dangerous, why did the FDA recommend its removal? One man in particular became passionate about thimerosal in vaccines. He was Robert F. Kennedy Jr., a well-known environmental activist and lawyer. His father, Robert F. Kennedy, had been a US senator and US attorney general. His uncle was President John F. Kennedy. Robert Kennedy Jr. believed that thimerosal could cause autism and brain damage, despite evidence to the contrary. By this time, in the early twenty-first century, news about Wakefield's study had crossed the Atlantic. Fears about thimerosal and the MMR vaccine blended together, and millions of US

At a press conference in Washington, DC, in 2008, Robert F. Kennedy Jr. discussed his belief that vaccines can cause harm. Because he comes from a famous political family, Kennedy has attracted a lot of attention to the anti-vaccination movement.

parents became terrified that vaccines could cause autism.

As these fears continued to take hold in the United States, they found another spokesperson in Jenny McCarthy, a Hollywood actor. Her three-year-old son, Evan, had starting showing signs of autism. In 2005, in an appearance on the *Oprah Winfrey Show*, McCarthy announced that Evan was autistic and that vaccines had caused his autism. She became an activist against vaccines and began holding rallies to promote safer vaccines with her boyfriend, actor Jim Carrey. Even though vaccines were already extremely safe, US vaccination rates began slipping.

In Britain, journalist Brian Deer spent seven years investigating Wakefield's history. From 2004 to 2011, Deer produced dozens of stories revealing that Wakefield had violated medical ethics guidelines, engaged in medical misconduct, and committed fraud. Specifically,

Wakefield had developed his own measles vaccine to launch when the public lost confidence in the MMR. He therefore stood to gain financially if parents switched from the MMR to his vaccine. He had also accepted money from a lawyer (who represented families who claimed the MMR caused harm) to show through research that the MMR was dangerous. Wakefield and the lawyer had even planned to find evidence of a new syndrome caused by the vaccine. In addition, Wakefield had not gotten proper consent from the parents of the children in his study. In fact, the lawyer paying Wakefield had sent these children to him for the study. Finally, Wakefield had altered and made up several numbers and other important details in the study.

Over the next several years, Wakefield's coauthors rejected the study. Deer earned a British Press Award for his investigation. In January 2010, Wakefield was found guilty of more than thirty charges, including twelve related to the abuse of children with developmental disabilities. The *Lancet* formally withdrew the study, and Wakefield lost his right to practice medicine. Yet the damage was done—Wakefield had successfully sowed seeds of doubt about the safety of vaccines. By then he had chosen to move from Britain to Austin, Texas, where he continues to promote the false belief that vaccines cause autism.

THE MEDIA AND FALSE BALANCE

Wakefield, McCarthy, Kennedy, and other activists did not cause fears about autism by themselves. The media played a part too. Newspapers, magazines, the Internet, and TV news shows reported the results of each new study showing no link between vaccines and autism. The news outlets also reported on activism against vaccines and some people's continued belief that vaccines caused autism. Faced with conflicting arguments, parents didn't know what to think.

Scientists had shown over and over that autism was not related to vaccines. In fact, more research has since begun to reveal that autism is largely a genetic disorder involving more than one hundred genes.

THE VACCINE "CONSPIRACY" THAT WASN'T

A conspiracy theory in 2014 breathed new life into the anti-vaccination movement. Brian Hooker, a biochemical engineer who believes that the MMR vaccine caused his son's autism, improperly reanalyzed data from a 2004 study coauthored by William Thompson, a CDC scientist. The study had shown no link between autism and vaccines, but Hooker claimed African American boys who received the MMR had a higher risk for autism.

Andrew Wakefield then posted a YouTube video claiming that the CDC had covered up research linking autism with vaccines. The video included a recorded conversation in which Thompson suggests that his 2004 study was flawed. Wakefield called Thompson a whistleblower within the CDC. A whistleblower is someone in an organization who "blows the whistle" by revealing corruption.

Thompson's coauthors stood by their work, and Hooker's paper was found to contain multiple problems. Later, autism blogger Matt Carey analyzed CDC documents that showed there was no cover-up. Despite this, Wakefield released a film in April 2016 promoting the CDC cover-up conspiracy. The film contains many factual errors and misinterpretations of research and dangerously misleads viewers.

It is present in babies before birth. But many journalists felt obligated to "report both sides" of the story each time they wrote about the vaccine controversy—even though one side was scientifically false. In many articles, they included research findings that vaccines did not cause autism but then quoted from parents or celebrities who believed they did. A few doctors believed in a vaccine-autism link, and journalists sometimes quoted them as well. But these doctors used treatments that were not supported by science or by major medical organizations.

Meanwhile, many websites promote "alternative medicines." Usually run by people without medical degrees, the sites claim that diseases can be cured "naturally," using vitamins, oils, herbal remedies, and other nontraditional approaches. Some sites argue that pharmaceutical medications, including vaccines, are harmful. They claim that in addition to autism, vaccines can cause other health problems, such as diabetes, allergies, sudden infant death syndrome, and cancer.

None of this is supported by scientific evidence. But in the first decade of the twenty-first century, more and more Americans were getting their news and information online. It was sometimes difficult to tell which sites were reliable. Parents searching for information about vaccines found contradictory results.

KNOWING TOO LITTLE TO KNOW BETTER

Many parents understandably want to research the benefits and risks of vaccines themselves But with so much misinformation online, someone without advanced scientific training could fall prey to the Dunning-Kruger effect, named for US social psychologists David Dunning and Justin Kruger.

By testing volunteers in specific skill areas and then asking them to estimate their own skill levels, the two scientists discovered that those with the lowest skill levels in a particular topic overestimated their abilities to master that topic, and those with the highest skill levels estimated their abilities accurately. These findings were not related to participants' intelligence. Rather, because of the Dunning-Kruger effect, those without advanced, specialized training in a topic—no matter how intelligent or otherwise educated they are—have difficulty accurately perceiving how much they really understand about that topic. So parents who want to research vaccines on their own—even highly intelligent and highly educated parents—are likely to inaccurately interpret vaccine studies because they lack specific expertise in vaccines. Without extensive experience studying vaccines, they cannot correctly recognize how well they understand technical vaccine research. In addition, dozens of anti-vaccine websites cite scientific studies but misrepresent the research.

Parents became increasingly nervous. Some asked pediatricians to skip some vaccines or space out their children's vaccines rather than follow the recommended CDC schedule. Even if they weren't convinced that vaccines caused autism, parents worried that children were getting too many vaccines too soon. They feared that vaccines would overwhelm their children's immune systems. The evidence-based reality is that not following the CDC schedule leaves children unprotected against disease for longer. Spreading out vaccines also involves more doctor visits, more medical bills, and more visits for children who might be afraid of needles. More doctor visits also increase the chance that patients will pick up germs in a doctor's waiting room.

NEW OUTBREAKS

Despite anti-vaccination fears, state governments require that children receive certain vaccines before starting school. States do allow some exceptions. For instance, children with a rare allergy to a vaccine ingredient can receive an exemption from immunization requirements. Most states allow exemptions based on religious beliefs. None of the major world religions—Hinduism, Buddhism, Judaism, Islam, and Christianity—officially rejects vaccination, but some small religious sects do oppose it. Some states also allow parents to exempt their children from vaccination requirements based on nonreligious "personal beliefs."

NVIC founder Barbara Loe Fisher wanted more states to allow vaccines exemptions for more reasons. The NVIC lobbied state and federal representatives to loosen vaccine requirements and let more parents opt out of vaccines for their children. NVIC recruited parents to testify about vaccines at state legislature hearings and gave misinformation about vaccines to lawmakers. The organization also gave parents information on how to more easily exempt their children from vaccine requirements. These efforts led to decreasing vaccination rates in some communities.

As the anti-vaccination movement in the United States grew, herd immunity began to break down in some places. In 2010, for example,

California experienced a massive pertussis outbreak with more than nine thousand cases, the most since 1959. Four years later, California had another pertussis outbreak of nearly ten thousand cases. The acellular pertussis vaccine had become less effective over time and was the biggest driver of these outbreaks. Research also showed that high rates of school vaccine exemptions in small areas had worsened the outbreaks. The real wake-up call came at the end of 2014, when measles arrived at Disneyland in Southern California. Already, 2014 had seen 667 cases of measles in twenty-seven states. This was the highest number in one year since measles had been eliminated (though not eradicated) from the United States in 2000. More than half of these cases came from a large outbreak in Ohio, mostly involving unvaccinated members of Amish communities. (The Amish are a Protestant group that rejects many aspects of the modern world, and some Amish communities don't vaccinate their children.)

The Ohio outbreak went largely unnoticed by the public. The Disneyland outbreak, however, dominated headlines and caused an uproar among parents and health-care professionals. Disneyland's reputation as a fun and safe family park clashed with the threat of a potentially deadly disease.

The Disneyland outbreak most likely started with a foreign visitor—the same measles strain had previously caused an outbreak in the Philippines. Measles moved quickly throughout California and other western states, especially in areas with lower vaccination rates. One study found that a community needs about 95 percent vaccination coverage to prevent measles transmission. But most communities with new measles cases had coverage rates below 86 percent. The outbreak sickened 131 people in California and 25 more in other states, Canada, and Mexico. Among those who got sick in California, 70 percent were unvaccinated. (No vaccine is 100 percent effective, and some of the infected individuals had received one measles vaccine dose but not the recommended two.)

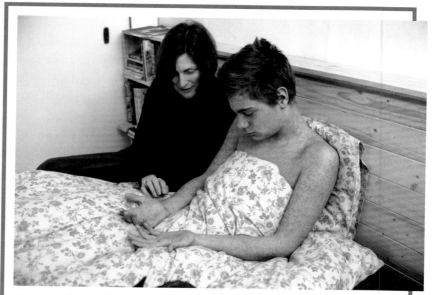

A teenage boy and his mother look at the measles rash on his body. Because he didn't get the measles vaccine as a baby, he was vulnerable to the disease when he encountered it as a teen. Although few people die of measles, they can develop serious complications, such as bronchitis, pneumonia, or inflammation of the brain.

The outbreak marked a sharp turn in attitudes toward vaccines in the United States. The media focused less on false balance—the effort to present "two sides of every story" even when one side is based on misinformation. Instead, most news coverage highlighted the public health danger posed by the rejection of vaccines. Many parents became enraged that vaccine refusals were putting the larger community, including those too young or too sick to be vaccinated, at risk.

THE LEGISLATIVE TIDE TAKES A TURN

The Disneyland outbreak motivated a group of California parents to push for stronger vaccination laws. Until the outbreak, all states except Mississippi and West Virginia allowed nonmedical vaccine exemptions, such as religious exemptions. The California parents, along with pediatrician and California state representative Richard

Pan, wanted California to eliminate nonmedical exemptions as well. Pan proposed the rule change with Senate Bill 277. The legislative fight was bitter. Some protesters who did not support the bill made exaggerated, nonsensical claims, suggesting that public health officials were killing people by forcing vaccinations. They charged that officials were treating them in the same way the German Nazi government treated Jewish Europeans during World War II. (The Nazis rounded up and murdered six million Jews, as well as homosexuals, disabled people, and others in concentration camps during the war.) Some parents gave tearful testimonies about children with injuries they believed were caused by vaccines. Others told of children who had died from vaccine-preventable diseases. Ultimately the law passed. Efforts in other states to tighten vaccination requirements built momentum as well.

A mother and her three children protest Senate Bill 277 in California. The bill, which passed in 2015 on the heels of the Disneyland measles outbreak, tightened vaccination requirements for California schoolchildren.

But failure to vaccinate continued to take a toll. In the spring of 2017, for example, a measles outbreak hit a community of immigrants from Somalia in Minneapolis, Minnesota. A decade earlier, the Somali community had higher MMR vaccination rates than the rest of Minnesota: 92 percent among Somali American two-year-olds compared to 88 percent statewide. But the Somali community in Minneapolis also had a much higher rate of autism with intellectual disability compared to the general population, for reasons scientists still do not understand. The rate was similar to that of white children in Minneapolis but with higher rates of intellectual disability. Andrew Wakefield and other anti-vaccine supporters targeted Somalis, spreading misinformation about the dangers of vaccines. So the MMR rate among Somali American children in Minnesota dropped, hitting 67 percent in 2009 and 42 percent in 2014. One month after the measles outbreak began in April 2017, sixty-six Minnesotans had been infected. Of these, fifty-seven were Somali and sixty-two had not been vaccinated.

Outbreaks like these occur partly because vaccines have become victims of their own success. Since they have largely wiped out polio, measles, tetanus, meningitis, and other infectious diseases in the United States, American parents don't know

It's very easy to catch measles from an infected person. For this reason, a health clinic in Minneapolis had visitors wear face masks for protection during a measles outbreak in 2017. The disease spread largely in the city's Somali community, where many parents had refused vaccinations for their children.

about or fear these diseases anymore. As vaccinologist Stanley Plotkin puts it, "The problem is that people pay less attention to something they *don't* see than things they *do* see, and they don't see as much disease."

But the Disneyland outbreak served as a reminder that infectious disease is not something of the past. It is not something to be denied or ignored. Ignoring it—and refusing vaccination—allows diseases to flourish, and to kill.

GLOBAL VACCINE RESISTANCE

Britain and the United States are not the only countries with citizens who oppose vaccines. Around the world, many communities have resisted vaccines. Their objections to vaccination have often been different from those of Americans and Europeans.

For example, the Roman Catholic Church is a powerful force around the world. The church opposes artificial birth control because it enables couples to have sex for pleasure and not just for procreation (making babies). Church leaders in some nations with large Catholic populations have suspected that WHO vaccinations were being used not to prevent disease but to keep women from having babies—a violation of church doctrine.

For instance, in the 1990s, rumors spread in Mexico, Venezuela, Tanzania, and the Philippines that a WHO tetanus vaccination campaign was really a way of secretly delivering birth control to women. A similar claim surfaced in 2014 in Kenya. There, a group of doctors and Catholic bishops claimed that the tetanus vaccine was being used to make women infertile to reduce overpopulation in Kenya. The doctor who started the rumors became suspicious of the vaccine partly because it was encouraged specifically for women between fifteen and forty-nine years old. This is the range of childbearing years. Some Kenyans were also suspicious because tests of the vaccine incorrectly revealed that it contained a hormone called human chorionic gonadotropin (hCG). This hormone had once been tested, but never used, in a vaccine designed to prevent pregnancy.

VACCINE DISASTERS

Vaccine tragedies are rare in the twenty-first century, especially in wealthy nations with strict vaccine regulations. But in poor or war-torn nations, which don't have the money or the resources to enforce strict rules, accidents happen.

In September 2014, three years after the start of civil war in Syria, a muscle relaxant called atracurium besylate got mixed up with saline used to dilute measles vaccines. This happened because the vials containing the substances looked similar. The confusion led to atracurium-contaminated vaccines that sickened seventy-five children and killed fifteen. In May 2015, two babies died and twenty-nine were hospitalized in Chiapas, Mexico. The hepatitis B vaccines they had received were contaminated with bacteria. And in the spring of 2016, a vaccine scandal rocked China. A pharmacist in the Chinese city of Heze sold more than two million doses of expired, improperly stored vaccines to medical clinics across China. Parents paid for the vaccines to protect their children from diseases not included in China's government-funded vaccination program. The vaccines did not sicken any children. However, vaccinologists say they might not be effective at preventing disease either.

Incidents like those in Syria, Mexico, and China have a double negative effect. First, the contaminated vaccines can harm or kill children who receive them. Second, vaccine disasters reduce trust in vaccination and other public health initiatives. This lack of trust can lead people to refuse vaccines, which opens the door for more disease, illness, and death.

The tetanus vaccine contained no hCG. It was given to women of childbearing age only to protect their newborns from the disease until the babies could get their first doses at six weeks old. Eventually the controversies were resolved and vaccination continued. Pregnancy and birth rates remained the same in Kenya and in other countries using the vaccine.

05

WHAT THE FUTURE MIGHT HOLD

Vaccinology has grown and changed immensely since Edward Jenner first inoculated James Phipps with cowpox. In the twenty-first century, vaccinologists fight disease using innovative technology, such as recombinant and conjugate vaccines. They are also working on new technologies, such as experimental DNA vaccines. Innovation is necessary because the pathogens vaccinologists are working to defeat are tricky and complex.

A TALE OF TWO TROPICAL DISEASES

A family in Sierra Leone (a country in West Africa) sleeps beneath mosquito netting, which keeps insects from biting them at night. Mosquito nets can help reduce malarial infections, but a vaccine is needed to more effectively fight the disease.

Two of the deadliest infectious diseases in the world are also two of the hardest for humans to fight. Malaria and dengue fever are transmitted by mosquito bites. About half the world's population is at risk for each disease. They occur in tropical regions, which have warm, wet weather much of the year. Mosquitoes breed in warm, standing water, and many types are most active at night.

Mosquitoes from the genus *Anopheles* carry the parasite that causes malaria. The parasite, a creature that survives by feeding off other living things, is a protozoan—a single-celled organism with both plantlike and animal-like characteristics. The protozoans that cause malaria belong to five different species, all in the genus *Plasmodium*. Two of these species, *P. falciparum* and *P. vivax*, cause most malaria illness and death. In 2015 malaria sickened an estimated 214 to 286 million people around the world and killed an estimated 438,000. In previous years, the numbers were even higher. Between 2010 and 2015, the global number of malaria infections dropped by 18 percent and malaria deaths were nearly cut in half.

The decrease came mostly from vector control—that is, reducing mosquito populations. Health officials reduce the number of mosquitoes in different ways. In some parts of the world, workers spray mosquito breeding grounds with powerful insecticides. They also distribute insecticide-treated nets to families, mostly in sub-Saharan Africa (south of the Sahara), where about 90 percent of malaria cases and deaths occur. Some types of mosquitoes are active at night, so people surround their beds with the nets, which prevent the insects from biting them when they sleep. Vector controls also include covering open windows with screens and cleaning up pools of standing water, where mosquitoes lay their eggs. Mosquito nets have helped the most in reducing infections. More than half the population at risk for malaria in sub-Saharan Africa slept under insecticide-treated nets in 2015, compared to only 5 percent of that population in 2005.

Vector control alone is not enough, however. "What makes [it] so difficult is that [mosquito larvae, or newly hatched mosquitoes] can live in a half an inch [1.3 cm] of water," said Gwen Pearson, an entomologist (scientist who studies insects) at Purdue University in Indiana. "That gives mosquitos many places to breed, especially in underdeveloped countries, where people have to haul their own water and have unpaved dirt roads. Muddy footprints are perfect for breeding."

Many mosquito species have developed resistance to insecticides, and some species of *Plasmodium* parasites have developed resistance to several antimalarial drugs. The sheer number of mosquito species carrying malaria (more than thirty) is daunting, since they all behave differently. Pearson explains, "Some like to feed inside houses, some outside. Some feed at night, others at dawn."

Workers try to control dengue fever with similar vector controls. Dengue is caused by a virus carried by the mosquito species *Aedes aegypti* and *Aedes albopictus*. An estimated 2.5 to 3.9 billion people in 128 countries are at risk for dengue. Unlike malaria, dengue cases have been increasing globally. In the Americas, much of Asia, Australia, and New Zealand, cases jumped from 1.2 million in 2008 to 2.2 million in 2010—and then to 3.2 million in 2015. Some of the increase in reported dengue cases stems from more data collection: when researchers look for more dengue cases, they usually find them.

CLIMATE CHANGE AND INFECTIOUS DISEASE

Around the world, temperatures are rising due to increases in the amount of heat-trapping carbon dioxide in Earth's atmosphere. Humans release carbon dioxide into the atmosphere when they burn fossil fuels (oil, coal, and natural gas).

Increasing global temperatures are changing rainfall patterns, creating droughts in some areas and strong storms in others. In regions with increased rainfall, mosquitoes have more pools of water in which to breed, and the insect's population goes up. Entomologist Gwen Pearson says that certain mosquitoes can also survive drought. "Aedes [dengue-carrying mosquito] eggs can withstand drying, so even if we have major rains followed by drought, the eggs can survive for months without water," she explains.

However, scientists don't know how climate change will affect the number of cases of diseases carried by mosquitoes. Many factors influence mosquito behavior and the behavior of the pathogens they carry. As the climate changes, those factors change too. For example, some evidence suggests that global warming may reduce the ability of *Plasmodium* parasites to cause malaria, no matter how many *Anopheles* mosquitoes or parasites exist.

Worldwide, an estimated 284 to 528 million dengue infections occur each year, but not all cause symptoms. About 25 percent of infected people experience symptoms, and 500,000 develop the most severe disease, called dengue hemorrhagic fever. Dengue is not as deadly as malaria, but it still kills an estimated 22,000 people every year.

Dengue-carrying mosquitoes bite mostly in the daytime, so bed nets cannot protect people all day. *A. aegypti* and *A. albopictus* also mostly live in cities, where people live close to one another in large populations. Cities are full of receptacles where rainwater can collect. "Something as small as a cap off a pop bottle is enough water for mosquitos to breed," Pearson said. "The warmer the water, the faster they develop."

A DENGUE VACCINE

The dengue virus is tricky. Four different serotypes (varieties) harm humans. A first infection with any serotype is often mild. However, the infected person develops immunity to only that serotype—not the other three. A second infection from a different serotype causes much more severe disease. In 2011 researchers tested a new dengue vaccine, called Dengvaxia, in more than ten thousand children between the ages of two and fourteen in Indonesia, Malaysia, Thailand, the Philippines, and Vietnam. The vaccine provided good immunity against two of the dengue serotypes but significantly lower protection for the other two. However, the third year after the children had been vaccinated, children ages two to five who received the vaccine were seven times more likely to be hospitalized for dengue than those who did not receive it. Scientists believe it's likely that fewer of these children had a previous dengue infection. The vaccine may have acted as a first infection without providing enough immunity against two serotypes. Therefore, children who later encountered one of those two serotypes got extremely sick—sicker than they would have been had they not been vaccinated at all.

Another clinical trial enrolled more than twenty thousand children between ages nine and sixteen in five Latin American countries. Dengue affected children of those ages more than any other people in those countries. No increased rates of dengue fever hospitalizations occurred in this trial. So in 2015 the pharmaceutical company Sanofi Pasteur received approval to use Dengvaxia in people between ages nine and forty-five.

Scientists continue to study vaccines after approval, and researchers analyzed the results from all these trials one year later. They concluded that Dengvaxia benefits individuals and the population in areas with high levels of dengue transmission. However, in areas with low transmission, hospitalization rates were higher, so the vaccine's risks may outweigh its benefits there. In areas with moderate dengue rates, the vaccine appears helpful overall, but hospitalization rates were still slightly increased.

Scientists are working on a new dengue vaccine, called TV003, which they hope will provide good protection against all four serotypes. With a better vaccine, it won't matter if someone hasn't yet had a first infection. He or she will be protected against severe dengue regardless of previous exposure and regardless of the serotype.

THE MALARIA PUZZLE

Malaria is even trickier than dengue. With most diseases, getting sick and then recovering provides immunity, preventing a person from getting future infections. That's not how malaria works. Those who get malaria develop only partial immunity. They can get malaria again and again, although the later infections might not be as severe. Since the disease itself doesn't provide full immunity, it is hard for vaccinologists to make a vaccine that provides full immunity. Vaccines work by triggering the body's natural immune response. But if the body doesn't have an effective response, how can a vaccine trigger it?

Developing an effective malaria vaccine is also difficult because the *Plasmodium* parasite lives inside two different hosts: humans and the two *Anopheles* mosquito species. The entire *Plasmodium* life cycle is complex, with about a dozen stages total. As a mosquito is biting a human, the parasite enters the human blood in the form of sporozoites. The sporozoites travel through the bloodstream to the liver. There they release thousands of merozoites. The merozoites leave the liver and infect red blood cells throughout the body. Once inside red blood cells, they reproduce. Then they burst out of the cells. As they burst out, they cause malaria's symptoms, including fever, headaches, muscle pain, and nausea. The new merozoites infect and burst out of more red blood cells. In the next round of development, some parasites inside the red blood cells grow into immature sexual cells called gametocytes. If

Malaria poses many obstacles for vaccinators because the parasite that causes the disease lives inside both human and mosquito hosts and takes a number of different forms during its life cycle. Here, an entomologist traps malaria-bearing mosquitoes for study in the Peruvian town of Lupuna.

another *Anopheles* mosquito bites an infected person, these gametocytes enter the mosquito's body. In the mosquito's gut, they reproduce, forming new sporozoites, which then travel to the mosquito's salivary glands to wait for the next human host.

Because *Plasmodium* changes form inside each host, it is difficult to target the parasite with a vaccine. In an experiment in 2002, vaccinologists tried targeting the sporozoite stage by exposing *Plasmodium*-infected mosquitoes to radiation. Human volunteers agreed to let the irradiated mosquitoes bite them to see what happened. The mosquitoes transmitted the sporozoites to the volunteers, but the sporozoites were too weak to do damage. The human immune system recognized the weakened sporozoites as intruders and mounted a defense for a future infection against malaria. The problem with this approach is that it is costly and impractical to catch millions of mosquitoes and expose them to radiation. A biotechnology company called Sanaria is exploring a more practical way to create vaccines using irradiated sporozoites.

Another malaria vaccine, RTS,S, received approval from European regulators in 2015 under the name Mosquirix. Made by GlaxoSmithKline, RTS,S targets a protein in sporozoites. That protein is too weak to stimulate the immune system on its own. So researchers fused it with a hepatitis B antigen—a way of "dressing up" an intruder so the immune system sees it better. The RTS,S vaccine works only against the species *P. falciparum*, the deadliest malaria parasite, responsible for about half of all malaria deaths. And a person must receive four doses for the vaccine to be effective. Three doses are given one month apart and another dose eighteen months later. The vaccine can only reduce the number of malaria episodes in a person instead of completely preventing the disease. In trials, RTS,S cut the percentage of total malaria episodes by one-quarter in children under five months old and by one-third in children five to seventeen months old. Instead of experiencing ten episodes of malaria, for example, a vaccinated infant experienced only seven or eight and a vaccinated toddler experienced only six or seven. However, most vaccination programs in Africa do not accommodate the RTS,S dosing schedule. So in 2016 the WHO began a pilot program in Ghana, Kenya, and Malawi to assess the vaccine schedule and the safety of the vaccine. The program will also assess how many lives the vaccine saves.

More than a dozen other malaria vaccines are in development, but none is as far along as RTS,S. One of these vaccines focuses on reducing transmission rather than preventing disease. First, a human receives a vaccine that causes the body to produce antibodies against the stage the parasite takes in a mosquito's gut. When a mosquito bites the vaccinated human and sips the blood, it takes up those antibodies. The antibodies then attack and kill the parasite inside the mosquito before it can reproduce and infect other humans. This approach doesn't prevent disease in the person who is vaccinated. However, it contributes to herd immunity by killing the parasite. When the mosquito bites another person, it won't infect that person.

Some malaria vaccines target the *Plasmodium* parasite at all life stages and have made it as far as Phase 2 trials. In fact, many scientists believe that targeting multiple life stages may be the best way forward. It will take a vaccine complex enough to match the parasite's complexity to truly make progress.

ZIKA: A NEW THREAT EMERGES

A baffling, disturbing trend started in April 2015: several regions of Brazil saw a sudden increase in babies born with microcephaly, or an abnormally small head. This birth defect usually results in a smaller-than-normal brain and lifelong disabilities. Children born with microcephaly may experience seizures, developmental delays, and intellectual and learning disabilities. They may also have problems with movement, balance, hearing seeing, or eating. No cure exists, and the health problems associated with microcephaly can lead to early death.

Congenital rubella—passed on from a mother who has rubella during pregnancy to her fetus—can cause microcephaly. Yet health officials had announced the elimination of this disease from the Americas around the same time the new microcephaly outbreak appeared. The culprit had to be something different.

Over the next several months, public health officials, epidemiologists, and other scientists pieced together the evidence. They eventually determined the cause to be the Zika virus. Zika is carried by the same mosquito species that carry dengue: *A. aegypti* (which also carries yellow fever) and *A. albopictus*. It can also be transmitted sexually. Researchers first discovered Zika in 1952 in a rhesus macaque monkey in Uganda. Two years later, doctors identified it for the first time in a human in Nigeria. But the disease remained rare. When it occurred in people, it caused only temporary fever, joint pain, irritated eyes, and a rash. Scattered cases in Africa and Asia never caused long-term problems.

Then a 2007 outbreak in Yap Island in the South Pacific Ocean turned into an epidemic. Multiple outbreaks spread across other South Pacific islands. This time, many people with the virus developed Guillain-Barré syndrome, a nerve disorder that can cause paralysis. The April 2015 outbreak of Zika exploded across South and Central America. Researchers believe that foreign visitors to Brazil, starting during the 2014 World Cup soccer competition, brought the disease with them.

The 2015 strain was more destructive than those before it.

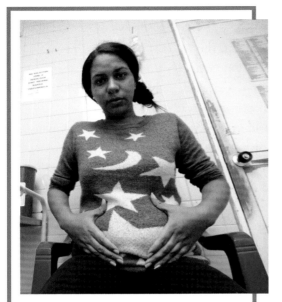

A vaccine to prevent Zika is urgently needed. Pregnant women with Zika, such as this mother-to-be in Colombia, can suffer miscarriages or stillbirths, or their babies might have severe and potentially fatal birth defects.

Researchers believe it mutated before or during its 2007 arrival in the Pacific. Some of the people infected in 2015 developed Guillain-Barré syndrome. Some infected pregnant women gave birth to babies with microcephaly and other birth defects. Other pregnant women had miscarriages or stillbirths (their babies died during pregnancy). Researchers have since learned much more about how the virus harms the fetus during pregnancy. The disease eventually spread through more than forty-five countries. In late July 2016, it reached the United States.

Vector control can partly manage Zika by reducing mosquito populations. But that is not a long-term solution. So research groups across the world almost immediately began working on a vaccine. By summer 2016, about eighteen governmental, medical, and educational institutions were working on possible vaccines, and the NIH had launched a Phase I clinical trial of a Zika vaccine with eighty healthy adults. In vaccine time, that's lightning fast. The NIH trial results showed the vaccine was safe and led to an immune response. As researchers continued tracking vaccine safety and effectiveness in trial participants for two years, the NIH started a Phase II trial for the same vaccine in March 2017. The Phase II trial aims to enroll 2,490 healthy adults in the United States and Puerto Rico, Brazil, Peru, Costa Rica, Panama, and Mexico—all areas where Zika infections occur. In that trial, researchers will determine the best dosing for the vaccine and continue evaluating its safety and effectiveness. Whether the world sees a Zika vaccine in a year or two, or ten or twenty, will depend on what scientists learn from those results. In the meantime, Zika cases in 2017 declined dramatically from 2016. But scientists warn that the disease will remain a threat for at least another decade.

THE WORLD'S MOST DIFFICULT DISEASE TO PREVENT

The number one killer of teenagers in Africa is acquired immune deficiency syndrome (AIDS), caused by the human immunodeficiency virus (HIV). Worldwide, AIDS is the number two killer of teens. In 2015, 2.1 million people contracted HIV and 1.1 million died from AIDS. HIV spreads through infected blood and through sexual intercourse. Mothers can also pass HIV to their babies during childbirth.

The AIDS epidemic began in the 1980s, and the FDA licensed the first AIDS drug in 1987. In 1996 a worldwide coalition launched the International AIDS Vaccine Initiative to develop a vaccine for HIV. Scientists estimate that a vaccine with even 70 percent effectiveness could prevent most new HIV infections each year by breaking the cycle of transmission. The fewer people who are infected, the fewer people they will infect.

In many ways, HIV presents the ultimate challenge in vaccine development. Inside the body, HIV reproduces billions of copies of itself in a single day, and all this copying results in many mutations. In this way, HIV evolves more rapidly than almost any other known organism. It is a moving target that is constantly changing its makeup.

Even more challenging, HIV attacks the very system the body uses to protect and defend itself: the immune system. The virus specifically attacks T-helper cells, the same cells that activate B cells to produce antibodies. Inside the T-helper cells, the virus replicates. Without enough healthy T-helper cells in the body, not enough B cells will produce antibodies to go after this and other viruses that may attack the body. (This is why doctors monitor the health of people with HIV by tracking their T cell counts.) Even if some B cells do make antibodies, those antibodies will attack the T-helper cells containing the virus. That's similar to soldiers attacking a dying general, the leader of the army. And because the virus mutates so rapidly, the body is often unable to produce antibodies quickly enough to recognize the latest version of the virus.

HIV REPLICATION

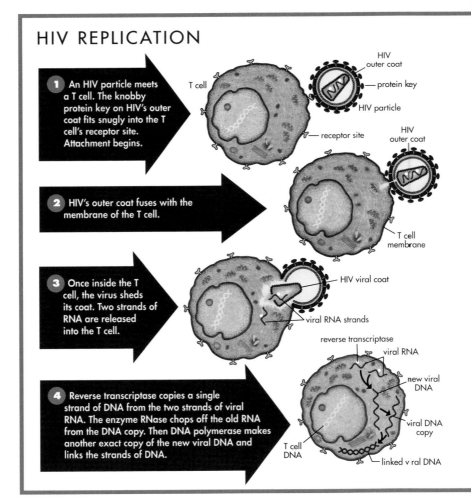

1. An HIV particle meets a T cell. The knobby protein key on HIV's outer coat fits snugly into the T cell's receptor site. Attachment begins.

T cell

HIV outer coat

protein key

HIV particle

receptor site

HIV outer coat

2. HIV's outer coat fuses with the membrane of the T cell.

T cell membrane

3. Once inside the T cell, the virus sheds its coat. Two strands of RNA are released into the T cell.

HIV viral coat

viral RNA strands

reverse transcriptase

viral RNA

new viral DNA

4. Reverse transcriptase copies a single strand of DNA from the two strands of viral RNA. The enzyme RNase chops off the old RNA from the DNA copy. Then DNA polymerase makes another exact copy of the new viral DNA and links the strands of DNA.

viral DNA copy

T cell DNA

linked viral DNA

The effort to develop an HIV vaccine has been frustrating. Since the virus was first discovered in 1983, researchers have tested only three HIV vaccines in humans. None of them has been effective.

Hope for an HIV vaccine emerged in late 2016 with the start of the first new trial in seven years. The HIV Vaccine Trials Network, a publicly funded international group, is conducting the trial. The vaccine candidate is called HVTN 702 in the lab. In the field, researchers call it Uhambo, which means "opportunity" in the African language Shona and "journey" in the African language Xhosa. The vaccine will be tested in fifty-four hundred young men and women in South Africa over

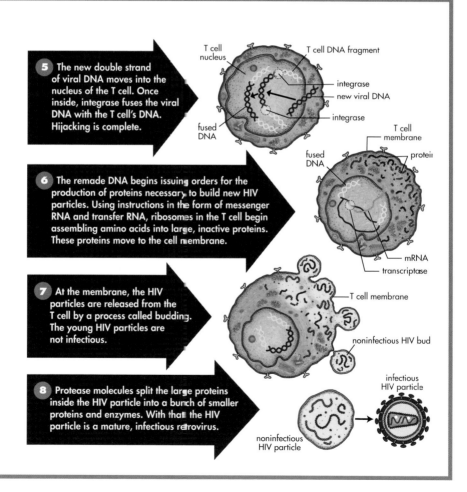

5 The new double strand of viral DNA moves into the nucleus of the T cell. Once inside, integrase fuses the viral DNA with the T cell's DNA. Hijacking is complete.

6 The remade DNA begins issuing orders for the production of proteins necessary to build new HIV particles. Using instructions in the form of messenger RNA and transfer RNA, ribosomes in the T cell begin assembling amino acids into large, inactive proteins. These proteins move to the cell membrane.

7 At the membrane, the HIV particles are released from the T cell by a process called budding. The young HIV particles are not infectious.

8 Protease molecules split the large proteins inside the HIV particle into a bunch of smaller proteins and enzymes. With that, the HIV particle is a mature, infectious retrovirus.

T cell nucleus
T cell DNA fragment
integrase
new viral DNA
integrase
fused DNA
T cell membrane
fused DNA
protein
mRNA
transcriptase
T cell membrane
noninfectious HIV bud
infectious HIV particle
noninfectious HIV particle

five years. HVTN 702 actually consists of two different experimental vaccines that were previously tested with some success in Thailand. The first is ALVAC-HIV. Made by the company Sanofi Pasteur, the vaccine is made from the canarypox virus, a disease in canaries that cannot infect humans. To create the vaccine, researchers used genetic engineering to insert three HIV proteins into the canarypox virus. These proteins are antigens that activate the T cells in the body and prime them to fight. The second vaccine, made by GlaxoSmithKline, is a subunit vaccine containing a genetically engineered protein from the surface of HIV. This vaccine boosts the immune response that has started and causes B cells to produce antibodies. Researchers hope that together the two vaccines will lead to an immune response that can prevent HIV infections. Researchers chose South Africa for testing because it has more citizens with HIV/AIDS than any other country in the world: approximately seven million people, or nearly one in every five adults. Participants will get five injections over a year, and researchers will follow them for two more years. Results are expected in 2020.

Meanwhile, other scientists continue working on other HIV vaccine strategies. Some are trying to develop DNA vaccines for HIV. This

DO WE NEED MORE STD VACCINES?

Sexually transmitted diseases are widespread in the United States. In 2015 doctors reported one and a half million new cases of chlamydia, four hundred thousand new cases of gonorrhea, and nearly twenty-four thousand new cases of syphilis—and the numbers are increasing.

In the past, these diseases were not high priorities for vaccine researchers. If an STD was detected early, antibiotics could treat it. But many bacteria have mutated, developing traits that make them resistant to antibiotics. Certain antibiotics that once easily killed bacteria that cause STDs are no longer very effective. Some are useless.

If doctors can't count on antibiotics to treat STDs, they will need to turn to vaccines. So vaccines for chlamydia, gonorrhea, and syphilis might soon became higher priorities for vaccine researchers.

work involves inserting a few HIV genes into a small piece of DNA used in the vaccine. Ideally, once in the body, those genes will produce proteins that are similar enough to proteins produced by HIV that the body will produce antibodies that can fight HIV. Other researchers are trying to use a type of virus called an adenovirus to carry fragments of HIV into the body that the researchers hope the immune system will attack. Deactivated adenoviruses are ideal for carrying genetic material in experimental vaccines. Researchers know that they are able to infect a wide range of human and animal tissues. And they are good for lab experiments because they can survive year-round for long periods outside a host. Researchers are also exploring oral HIV vaccines as well as vaccines that can be injected into the skin instead of the muscle.

EBOLA OUTBREAK

In late December 2013, an eighteen-month-old boy died in a small village in Guinea, a country in West Africa. No one at the time knew what disease he had, but it soon spread to nearby nations. Although it's not certain that the toddler was the first case, he was among those who spawned the worst epidemic of Ebola disease since its discovery in 1976. The outbreak, which ended in 2016, claimed 11,325 lives among the more than 28,600 people who contracted the disease.

Ebola disease is devastating and often fatal. Once the virus gets into the body, it eventually infects and destroys nearly every cell type. At first, the victim experiences flu-like symptoms, such as fever, aches, headaches, and fatigue. Symptoms then progress to severe internal bleeding. About half of those infected with Ebola virus die; scientists aren't sure why some survive and others don't.

During the 2013–2016 outbreak, scientists developed a treatment called ZMapp, which contains antibodies against Ebola virus. ZMapp differs from a vaccine because it does not cause the immune system to create antibodies. Instead, it provides passive immunity; a person is injected with already produced antibodies that immediately attack

Health workers in the African nation of Guinea transport a patient to an Ebola treatment center. To keep the virus from entering their bodies, the workers wear protective gear from head to toe.

the virus. ZMapp was a controversial emergency measure during the 2013–2016 outbreak because it had not been studied for safety or effectiveness.

Scientists wanted to develop a vaccine to prevent future Ebola outbreaks instead of treating cases with an untested drug. The need was urgent. The outbreak had ravaged Guinea, Liberia, and Sierra Leone and had sickened two US nurses and a Spanish nurse who had cared for West African travelers. With Ebola threatening the United States and Europe, research agencies suddenly fast-tracked vaccines that had been partly developed or tested only in animals.

Of the five known species of Ebola, *Zaire ebolavirus* is the deadliest. It was the one responsible for the 2013–2016 outbreak. So vaccine developers focused on that strain. Several very different vaccines emerged as top candidates and entered Phase 2 trials during 2015.

The Ebola virus has many challenges for vaccine developers. First, one of its major proteins can take one of three different shapes. This flexibility increases the amount of damage the virus can do to the body. In addition, the Ebola virus blocks the body's release of interferon, a protein that alerts the immune system to a foreign pathogen. Finally, carbohydrates make up half the virus's mass and cloak it in a sort of disguise. Since the human body uses carbohydrates for energy, the virus doesn't look foreign to the immune system.

The speediness and global cooperation of vaccine manufacturers paid off. By the end of 2016, an Ebola vaccine called rVSV-ZEBOV was in hand. A trial of almost twelve thousand participants in Guinea and Sierra Leone throughout 2015 and 2016 found that no one who received the vaccine developed Ebola virus disease. Those findings suggest that the vaccine is 100 percent effective, but several difficulties in the trial make it hard to know for sure, and the journey isn't over. More studies have to confirm the vaccine's safety and effectiveness. And no one knows how long immunity from the vaccine lasts or whether its design can be used to make vaccines for other Ebola species. The pharmaceutical company Merck is conducting more safety studies and submitted the vaccine to the FDA for approval in late 2017.

WHAT'S NEXT?

In addition to vaccines for malaria, dengue, Zika, and Ebola, researchers are working on vaccines for other diseases as well. One is respiratory syncytial virus (RSV), the most common cause of lower respiratory tract infections in children. Every year in the United States, RSV causes 75,000 to 125,000 hospitalizations, a half million emergency room visits, two hundred to five hundred deaths in infants, and ten thousand to fourteen thousand deaths in the elderly. In poor nations, sixty-six thousand to two hundred thousand children die each year from RSV.

Scientists are also exploring vaccine development for skin diseases caused by herpes viruses. Then there is tuberculosis (TB), a disease that damages the lungs. World health workers refer to TB, malaria, and HIV as the "big three" diseases because together they account for 10 percent of all deaths worldwide. An existing vaccine for TB isn't very effective; scientists want a better one. Vaccines already exist for hepatitis A and B, and in 2015 Chinese vaccinologists developed one for hepatitis E. But we still don't have vaccines for two other life-threatening types of hepatitis—C and D.

An entirely different type of research focuses on cancer vaccines.

VACCINES DURING PREGNANCY

Pregnancy may be an ideal time to prevent diseases that can harm a fetus or newborn. Zika and rubella are examples of infectious diseases that cause birth defects. Another is cytomegalovirus, a leading cause of nongenetic deafness and other birth defects, including intellectual disability.

Cytomegalovirus is extremely common. It infects almost one in three children by the age of five and half of all adults by middle age (forties and fifties). It rarely causes symptoms or problems. However, if a woman becomes infected during pregnancy, her child is at higher risk for birth defects. An estimated forty thousand babies are born each year with the infection, and one in five will have deafness, intellectual difficulties, or similar problems. Scientists are working on a vaccine to prevent cytomegalovirus infections to reduce these birth defects. Women might receive the vaccine in childhood or before or during pregnancy.

One in four healthy adult women are infected with bacteria called group B streptococcus. Group B strep does not cause health problems for an infected woman, but she can pass the infection to her newborn. About one in two thousand newborns develop complications from a group B strep infection. These can include breathing problems, pneumonia (infection of the lungs), swelling in the brain and spinal cord, heart problems, and kidney problems. A group B strep vaccine could prevent these serious complications. A Phase 2 study in 2016 showed promising results for a safe, effective vaccine, but scientists must conduct more trials to confirm those results.

RSV does not affect a fetus, but it is the leading cause of pneumonia and inflammation in the lungs in children under the age of one. Scientists have struggled to develop a vaccine against RSV for decades. One research direction involves developing an RSV vaccine for pregnant women instead of newborns, whose immune systems may not be mature enough to respond adequately to certain vaccines. Women already receive pertussis and influenza vaccines during pregnancy so that their bodies will produce antibodies that pass on to the fetus. Those maternal antibodies offer newborns protection against pertussis and flu for several months after birth. An RSV vaccine could work the same way.

A scientist at the National Institutes of Health studies a map of the DNA of the hepatitis C virus. The more scientists can learn about the genetic makeup of a disease, the better they can tailor a vaccine to prevent that disease.

Nearly all existing vaccines are prophylactic, which means they prevent disease. Both the HPV and hepatitis B vaccines prevent cancer by preventing the viral infections that can cause the cancer. Researchers also want to develop therapeutic vaccines to treat existing cancers. These vaccines would strengthen the body's immune response by teaching T cells to fight the cancer or by producing antibodies that would bind to the surface of cancer cells and kill them. The FDA has approved only one therapeutic vaccine, against a type of prostate cancer. Others are in development and testing stages.

Which vaccine will scientists develop next? Will the world ever see a vaccine that effectively prevents malaria or HIV? What inevitable new pathogen will appear and set scientists rushing to the lab to brainstorm a new vaccine?

For more than one million years, humans and microorganisms have been locked in a never-ending battle. Using variolation and then vaccination, humans have tried to outsmart pathogens. But almost as quickly, new pathogens have evolved, mutating and thereby staying one step ahead of vaccine developers. The world will likely never run out of organisms that sicken and kill humans. We humans will need a constant supply of clever scientists who keep fighting back with vaccines. Maybe you will be one of them.

SOURCE NOTES

4–5 James Cherry, telephone conversation with author, December 26, 2016.

17 Tara Haelle, "Is the Most Terrifying Measles Complication More Common Than We Thought?," *Forbes*, October 30, 2016, http://www.forbes.com/sites /tarahaelle/2016/10/30/is-the-most-terrifying-measles-complication-more -common-than-we-thought/#5feafbe64936.

32–33 S. L. Kotar and J. E. Gessler, *Smallpox: A History* (Jefferson, NC: McFarland, 2013), 69.

35 Tara Haelle, "Polio Vaccine Found 'Safe and Effective' 60 Years Ago: What Would Salk Think Today?," *Forbes*, April 13, 2015, http://www.forbes.com/sites /tarahaelle/2015/04/13/polio-vaccine-found-safe-and-effective-60-years-ago -what-would-salk-think-today/#37412b2562ac.

36 Roy Gibbons, "Tests Show Drug Works in 80-90% of Cases," *Chicago Tribune*, April 13, 1955, http://archives.chicagotribune.com/1955/04/13/page/1/article /salk-vaccine-called-safe-effective.

36 Haelle, "Polio Vaccine Found 'Safe and Effective.'"

41 Sona Bari, telephone conversation with author, January 6, 2017.

42 Ayodele Samuel Jegede, "What Led to the Nigerian Boycott of the Polio Vaccination Campaign?," *PLoS Medicine*, March 20, 2007, http://journals.plos .org/plosmedicine/article?id=10.1371/journal.pmed.0040073.

43 Arsla Jawaid, "Pakistan's Polio Workers Targeted for Killing," *Al-Jazeera*, December 17, 2013, http://www.aljazeera.com/indepth/features/2013/12 /pakistan-polio-workers-targeted-killing-201312118364851379.html?utm=from _old_mobile.

43 Ibid.

45 Stanley Plotkin, telephone conversation with author, December 21, 2016.

45–46 Michael Shea, "The Long Road to an Effective Vaccine for Meningococcus Group B (MenB)," *Annals of Medical Surgery*, June 15, 2013, 53.

46 Plotkin, telephone conversation.

49 Paul Offit, telephone conversation with author, December 19, 2016.

50 Laura Newman, "Maurice Hilleman," *BMJ*, April 30, 2005, 1028.

50 Offit, telephone conversation.

51 Ibid.

56 Tara Haelle, "It's Past Time for Lyme Disease Vaccine, Says Vaccine Developer Stanley Plotkin," *Forbes*, September 8, 2016, http://www.forbes .com/sites/tarahaelle/2016/09/08/its-past-time-for-lyme-disease-vaccine-says -vaccine-developer-stanley-plotkin/#2bec01133ef0.

57 Carolyn G. Shapiro-Shapin, "Pearl Kendrick, Grace Eldering, and the Pertussis Vaccine," *Emerging Infectious Disease*, August 2010, https://www.ncbi.nlm.nih .gov/pmc/articles/PMC3298325/.

61 John Schiller, telephone conversation with author, January 4, 2017.

62 Ibid.

66 "Jacobson v. Massachusetts 197 U.S. 11 (1905)," Justia, accessed July 18, 2017, https://supreme.justia.com/cases/federal/us/197/11/case.html.

68 M. Best, A. Katamba, and D. Neuhauser, "Making the Right Decision: Benjamin Franklin's Son Dies of Smallpox in 1736," *Quality and Safety in Health Care* 16, no. 6 (December 2007): 478.

70 Offit, e-mail to author, January 3, 2017.

72 "Update on the National Vaccine Injury Compensation Program (VICP)," HRSA, June 6, 2012, https://www.hhs.gov/sites/default/files/nvpo/nvac /meetings/pastmeetings/2012/evans_062512.pdf.

73 Dorit Rubinstein Reiss, "HPV Vaccine Consent Case in New York—a Review," *Skeptical Raptor*, March 9, 2017, https://www.skepticalraptor.com /skepticalraptorblog.php/hpv-vaccine-consent-case-new-york-review/.

77 "Timeline: Thimerosal in Vaccines (1999–2010)," CDC, last modified August 28, 2015, https://www.cdc.gov/vaccinesafety/concerns/thimerosal/timeline.html.

87 Plotkin, telephone conversation.

91 Gwen Pearson, telephone conversation with author, January 15, 2017.

91 Ibid.

92 Pearson, telephone conversation with author, July 16, 2017.

92–93 Ibid.

GLOSSARY

acellular vaccine: a vaccine that contains material from cells, such as proteins, but not complete cells. Acellular vaccines are not as effective over time as whole-cell vaccines.

antibodies: proteins created by the immune system that attack antigens. The immune cells create specific antibodies to fight specific antigens.

antigen: a substance on the surface of a virus, bacterium, or other pathogen that the immune system recognizes as an invader

antigenic drift: small mutations in a virus's genes that occur during replication. The influenza virus frequently undergoes antigenic drift, requiring creation of a new flu vaccine each year.

antigenic shift: a major change in a virus's composition, resulting from sudden and large genetic mutations. Antigenic shift can occur in influenza when the virus jumps from a nonhuman species to humans or when two different strains of flu infect one organism at the same time.

antitoxins: antibodies that can cancel the effects of toxins produced by bacteria that cause disease. An antitoxin treats infection caused by a bacterial toxin.

bacteria: simple, single-celled organisms found in soil, air, water, and living things. Some bacteria cause disease.

cognitive biases: ways of thinking that can lead to illogical conclusions

conjugate vaccine: a vaccine containing a coating from bacteria that the immune system does recognize and an antigen that the immune system does recognize. When it attacks the antigen, the immune system also learns to attack the coating.

contagious disease: a disease that one person can get from contact with another through casual touch, sexual activity, or exchange of bodily fluids

deoxyribonucleic acid (DNA): double-stranded molecules inside cells that hold instructions for how an organism will grow, reproduce, and function

DNA vaccines: experimental vaccines containing genes with instructions for making antigens. Once inside the body, the genes show other cells how to make the antigens.

elimination: the removal of a disease from a geographical area so that it no longer circulates there on its own

epidemic: a collection of outbreaks of a disease that lead to more cases than would normally be expected

epidemiology: the study of what can cause or prevent a disease, where it occurs, how often it occurs, how it spreads, and whom it affects

eradication: removal of a disease from the entire planet, so that it no longer infects any humans. For a disease to be considered eradicated, it must be eliminated from all regions on Earth.

evolution: the gradual change in a species' genetic makeup over time. This results from random genetic mutations and from mutations that enable an organism to better survive in its environment.

fungus: an organism that reproduces using spores and feeds on organic matter. Examples include molds, mushrooms, and yeast.

genes: chemicals that carry instructions for how each living thing will grow, function, and reproduce. Genes are found on strands of DNA.

genetic engineering: manipulating genes to change an organism's characteristics. Scientists use genetic engineering to create some kinds of vaccines.

germ theory: the idea that microscopic organisms cause disease. French chemist Louis Pasteur and German physician Robert Koch developed the germ theory of disease in the late nineteenth century.

herd immunity: protection against a specific disease for most members of a community created by high vaccination rates. Herd immunity protects individuals who are not vaccinated because it lowers the number of disease carriers. With fewer disease carriers, a disease is less likely to spread.

immune system: a system of cells, tissues, and organs that work together to protect the body from disease. Vaccines trigger the immune system to prepare defenses against specific diseases.

immunity: the ability to resist a particular disease because one's immune system has already encountered the disease and knows how to fight it. A person can develop immunity either by surviving a disease infection or by getting a vaccine that triggers the immune system to prepare defenses against the disease.

inactivated vaccine: a vaccine that contains a pathogen that has been killed or made ineffective. Inactivated pathogens cannot replicate inside the body or cause disease, but they still trigger the immune system to create defenses against them.

infectious disease: a disease that occurs when a pathogen, such as a virus, bacterium, or parasite, enters the body. Pathogens can enter the body in a number of ways, such as person-to-person contact, an insect bite, or through a cut on the skin.

live attenuated vaccine: a vaccine made of a weakened form of a virus or bacterium. The vaccine triggers an immune response in the body but is too weak to cause harm.

mutation: a change in an organism's genetic makeup that can be passed on to future generations. Because pathogens sometimes mutate, vaccinologists must reformulate vaccines to make them effective against the changed organism.

pandemic: an outbreak of a disease that occurs over a wide geographic area and infects an unusually large proportion of individuals

parasite: an organism that survives by feeding from or otherwise depending on a host. An example is *Plasmodium*, a single-celled organism that lives inside both mosquitoes and humans. *Plasmodium* is responsible for malaria.

passive immunity: temporary immunity to a disease provided by antibodies created outside the body. The antibodies can be created in a laboratory or taken from another person. A pregnant woman also naturally transfers antibodies to her fetus.

pathogen: a virus, bacteria, fungus, parasite, or other agent that causes disease

recombinant vaccines: vaccines made using genetic engineering. During this process, genes from a pathogen are altered or combined with another organism or with another organism's genes.

rotavirus: a virus that causes diarrhea and other symptoms, especially in children. The virus can pass from person to person through contaminated food, water, or human feces.

subunit vaccines: vaccines that contain only pieces of a pathogen, usually proteins. These proteins alone can stimulate the immune system to fight the pathogen.

toxoid vaccines: vaccines containing a substance called a toxoid, which remain when toxins in bacteria are deactivated. A toxoid in a vaccine triggers an immune reaction against the toxin but does not make the person sick.

vaccine: a human-made biological agent that triggers the immune system to develop defenses against a particular disease. Vaccines are made of the same pathogens they are meant to protect against. They do not harm the body because the pathogens within them have been weakened or killed.

variolation: infecting someone with variola minor, a mild form of smallpox, to trigger immunity against deadlier forms of smallpox. Healers used variolation to protect patients from smallpox in the years before Edward Jenner developed a smallpox vaccine containing cowpox in 1796.

virus: a microscopic pathogen that reproduces only after it has infected a living cell

SELECTED BIBLIOGRAPHY

Armstrong, Gregory, Laura Conn, and Robert Pinner. "Trends in Infectious Disease Mortality in the United States during the 20th Century." *JAMA* 281, no. 1 (January 6, 1999): 61–66.

Behbehani, A. "The Smallpox Story: Life and Death of an Old Disease." *Microbiological Reviews* 47, no. 4 (December 1983): 11.

Deer, Brian. "Exposed: Andrew Wakefield and the MMR-Autism Fraud." Briandeer. com. Accessed May 29, 2017. http://briandeer.com/mmr/lancet-summary.htm.

Mnookin, Seth. *The Panic Virus: The True Story behind the Vaccine-Autism Controversy.* New York: Simon & Schuster, 2012.

Myers, Martin, and Diego Pineda *Do Vaccines Cause That?! A Guide for Evaluating Vaccine Safety Concerns.* Galveston, TX: Immunizations for Public Health, 2008.

Offit, Paul. *The Cutter Incident: How America's First Polio Vaccine Led to the Growing Vaccine Crisis.* New Haven, CT: Yale University Press, 2005.

———. *Deadly Choices: How the Anti-Vaccine Movement Threatens Us All.* New York: Basic Books, 2011.

———. *Vaccinated: One Man's Quest to Defeat the World's Deadliest Diseases.* New York: Harper Collins, 2007.

Plotkin, Stanley, ed. *History of Vaccine Development.* New York: Springer, 2011.

"Vaccines and Immunizations." Centers for Disease Control and Prevention. Last modified April 21, 2017. http://www.cdc.gov/vaccines/index.html.

Wood, David, and Philip Brunell. "Measles Control in the United States: Problems of the Past and Challenges for the Future." *Clinical Microbiology Reviews* 8, no. 2 (April 1995): 260–267.

FURTHER INFORMATION

BOOKS

Allen, Arthur. *Vaccine: The Controversial Story of Medicine's Greatest Lifesaver.* New York: W. W. Norton, 2007.

Biss, Eula. *On Immunity: An Inoculation.* Minneapolis: Graywolf, 2015.

Conis, Elena. *Vaccine Nation: America's Changing Relationship with Immunization.* Chicago: University of Chicago Press, 2014.

Goldsmith, Connie. *Battling Malaria: On the Front Lines against a Global Killer.* Minneapolis: Twenty-First Century Books, 2011.

———. *The Ebola Epidemic: The Fight, the Future.* Minneapolis: Twenty-First Century Books, 2016.

Henderson, Donald A. *Smallpox: The Death of a Disease.* Amherst, NY: Prometheus Books, 2009.

Hirsch, Rebecca E. *The Human Microbiome. The Germs That Keep You Healthy.* Minneapolis: Twenty-First Century Books, 2017.

Jacobs, Charlotte DeCroes. *Jonas Salk: A Life.* New York: Oxford University Press, 2015.

Kallen, Stuart A. *The Race to Discover the AIDS Virus: Luc Montagnier vs. Robert Gallo.* Minneapolis: Twenty-First Century Books, 2013.

Kirkland, Anna. *Vaccine Court: The Law and Politics of Injury.* New York: New York University Press, 2016.

Marrin, Albert. *Very, Very, Very Dreadful: The Influenza Pandemic of 1918.* New York: Knopf Books for Young Readers, 2018.

McNeil, Donald G., Jr. *Zika: The Emerging Epidemic.* New York: W. W. Norton, 2016.

Rosen, George. *A History of Public Health.* Baltimore: Johns Hopkins University Press, 2015.

Shah, Sonia. *Pandemic: Tracking Contagions, from Cholera to Ebola and Beyond.* New York: Sarah Crichton Books, 2016.

Wadman, Meredith. *The Vaccine Race: Science, Politics, and the Human Costs of Defeating Disease.* New York: Viking, 2017.

FILMS

Haelle, Tara. "Why Parents Fear Vaccines." YouTube video, 12:49. Posted by "TEDx Talks," May 2, 2015. https://www.youtube.com/watch?v=ggtkzkoI3eM. Tara Haelle, the author of this book, explains why some parents refuse to vaccinate their children and the threat to public health that results.

Hilleman: A Perilous Quest to Save the World's Children. DVD. Haverford, PA: Medical History Pictures, 2016.
   US microbiologist Maurice Hilleman created more than forty vaccines in the mid-twentieth century. This documentary film describes his lifesaving work.

Invisible Threat. Carlsbad, CA: chatvFILMS, 2014. https://vimeo.com/ondemand /invisiblethreat.
   Produced by an award-winning high school broadcast journalism and documentary film program, this documentary explores vaccine science and the fears and misconceptions surrounding vaccine hesitancy and refusal.

Someone You Love: The HPV Epidemic. DVD. Philadelphia: Lumiere Media, 2014.
   This excellent documentary tells the story of a young woman who develops cervical cancer, a disease the HPV vaccine can prevent.

Vaccines: Calling the Shots. DVD. Arlington, VA: Public Broadcasting Service, 2014.
   This documentary film examines the threat of infectious diseases, the science behind vaccinations, and the risks of disease outbreaks caused by vaccine refusal.

"The War against Microbes." Nobelprize.org, 2012. http://www.nobelprize.org /mediaplayer/index.php?id=1524.
   This half-hour documentary explores the history and science behind the fight against infectious diseases.

WEBSITES

American Academy of Pediatrics (AAP)
   https://www.healthychildren.org/English/safety-prevention/immunizations /Pages/Immunizations-for-Teenagers-and-Young-Adults.aspx
   This professional organization of pediatricians provides information and resources about the vaccines recommended for infants, children, adolescents, and young adults.

Bill and Melinda Gates Foundation
   http://www.gatesfoundation.org/
   Microsoft founder Bill Gates and his wife, Melinda, created this philanthropic organization, whose guiding principle is "All lives have equal value." One of the foundation's biggest programs involves vaccine research and increasing immunization around the world.

Centers for Disease Control and Prevention (CDC)
   http://www.cdc.gov/vaccines/index.html
   The job of this federal US agency is to improve and maintain the physical and mental health of all Americans and to work to prevent diseases. The CDC regularly reviews research on vaccines, makes official vaccine recommendations for the United States, and carries out studies that test the safety and effectiveness of vaccines.

Children's Hospital of Philadelphia (CHOP) Vaccine Education Center
http://www.chop.edu/centers-programs/vaccine-education-center
CHOP's Vaccine Education Center provides current and accurate information about vaccines, including their safety, ingredients, benefits, and risks. The center also uses videos, information sheets, e-mail newsletters, webinars, and speaker programs to correct misinformation about vaccines.

Every Child by Two (ECBT)
http://www.vaccinateyourfamily.org/
http://www.ecbt.org/
http://shotofprevention.com/
Founded in 1991 by former US first lady Rosalynn Carter and Betty Bumpers, a former first lady of Arkansas, ECBT was largely responsible for state laws that require vaccines for schoolchildren. In the twenty-first century, ECBT focuses on educating parents and policy makers about vaccines, raising public awareness about vaccine benefits, ensuring that all families have access to vaccines, and advocating for policies that support vaccination.

Immunization Action Coalition (IAC)
http://www.vaccineinformation.org/
The IAC creates educational materials about vaccines and works to increase vaccination rates. The organization works with health-care groups, government health agencies, and others to improve communication with patients and parents.

National Foundation for Infectious Diseases
http://www.nfid.org/
This nonprofit organization works to educate the public and health-care professionals about vaccines and about the causes, prevention, and treatment of infectious diseases.

TeensHealth
http://kidshealth.org/en/teens/immunizations.html
This site offers an overview of vaccinations recommended for teenagers and answers to commonly asked questions about them.

Voices for Vaccines
http://www.voicesforvaccines.org/
Voices for Vaccines provides straightforward information about vaccines based on scientific evidence.

World Health Organization (WHO)
http://www.who.int/topics/vaccines/en/
WHO is the largest health organization in the world, with offices in more than 150 countries. WHO sets global health priorities, coordinates immunization campaigns across the world, and works with governments to improve and maintain the health of all individuals across the world. WHO moves quickly to address health threats, such as Ebola outbreaks, and collaborates with international partners to improve access to vaccines for all children.

INDEX

acellular vaccines, 56, 58, 83

animal testing of vaccines, 45–46, 47, 104

antibodies, 12–13, 15, 23, 36, 55, 58, 59, 63, 67, 96, 100–102, 103, 106, 107

antigenic drift, 53–54

antigenic shift, 53–54

antigen presenters, 12, 14

antigens, 12–13, 14–15, 16, 19, 21–23, 59, 95, 102

autism vaccine controversy, 74–82, 86

bin Laden, Osama, 41–42

binomial nomenclature, 22

Centers for Disease Control and Prevention (CDC), 9, 25–26, 51, 55–56, 58, 60, 62–63, 72, 74, 80, 82

chickenpox, 6–7

vaccine for, 16, 20, 26, 50

climate change, 92

cocooning, 16, 58

cognitive bias, 68–69

conjugate vaccines, 22, 89

contagiousness of diseases, 6, 18, 29, 34, 37, 57, 66

correlation and causation, 76

Deer, Brian, 78–79

dengue, 90–92, 93–94, 97, 105

vaccine for, 10

deoxyribonucleic acid (DNA), 21–22, 23, 32, 41, 52–53, 89, 101, 102

Department of Health and Human Services, 48, 71

diphtheria, tetanus, pertussis vaccines, 24–26, 56, 58, 70–71

DNA vaccines, 22, 89, 102

Dunning-Kruger effect, 81

Ebola, 6, 103–105

outbreaks of, 49

vaccine for, 49

Eldering, Grace, 56, 57

elimination of a disease, 43, 74, 97

eradication of a disease, 38, 39, 41–43

evolution, 32, 51–52, 99, 107

Fisher, Barbara Loe, 70–71, 73, 82

Food and Drug Administration (FDA), 38, 46, 48, 55, 58, 61, 71, 72, 77, 99, 105, 107

Franklin, Benjamin, 68

genes, 12, 21–23, 32, 51–54, 70, 79, 103–106

genetic engineering, 21, 23, 102

genetic mutations, 51, 53

germ theory, 27–28, 33

hepatitis, 26, 65

vaccines for, 16, 21, 23–24, 41, 49–51, 88, 95, 105

herd immunity, 16, 18, 19, 58, 82, 96

Hilleman, Maurice, 49–51, 53–54, 62

HIV/AIDS, 10, 17, 32, 42, 99–103, 105, 107

vaccine for, 10, 99, 101–103

human papillomavirus (HPV), 61, 63

vaccine for, 21, 26, 62, 73

immune cells, 12–13, 16

immune system, 7–17, 19–23, 26, 44–45, 55, 58–59, 61, 64, 67, 74, 82, 95–96, 99, 103–104, 106

immunity, 6, 8, 13, 16, 18, 19, 21, 23, 29, 34, 53–54, 58, 59, 82, 93, 94, 96, 105

inactivated vaccine, 19, 21, 24, 37, 38, 57

infectious disease, 5–8, 9–11, 34, 86–87, 90, 106
influenza, 7, 32, 52–54
    pandemic of 1918–1919, 53–54
    vaccine for, 10, 21–22, 106
infographics, 14–15, 18, 25, 101
iron lung, 4, 34

Jenner, Edward, 31–33, 64–65, 89

Kendrick, Pearl, 56–57
Kennedy, Robert F., Jr., 77, 79
Koch, Robert, 33

live attenuated vaccines, 20, 24
Lyme disease, 54–55
    vaccine for, 54–56

malaria, 7, 8, 39, 90–91, 92, 94–96, 105
    vaccine for, 10, 94–97, 105
McCarthy, Jenny, 78, 79
measles, 5, 6, 7, 9, 16, 17, 26, 43, 52, 56, 68, 73–74, 83
    outbreaks of, 6, 16, 49–50, 67, 73–74, 83–84, 86
    vaccines for, 16, 24, 26, 59, 74, 78, 79, 88
measles-mumps-rubella (MMR) vaccine, 16, 25
meningococcal disease, 5, 7, 22, 26, 49–50, 55, 86
mosquito-borne illnesses, 8–10, 90–98
mumps, 6–7, 43, 51
    vaccine for, 16, 25, 49–51, 67

National Childhood Vaccine Injury Act, 71
National Foundation for Infantile Paralysis, 35
National Institutes of Health (NIH), 61, 98

National Vaccine Information Center (NVIC), 73, 82
National Vaccine Injury Compensation Program, 72

passive immunity, 59, 103
Pasteur, Louis, 33
pertussis, 6, 7, 26, 56, 57, 58, 67, 83
    vaccine for, 19, 21, 24, 56, 57, 58–59, 67, 83
polio, 4–9, 26, 34–39, 42–43, 67, 86
    epidemics of, 34–35
    vaccine for, 20, 24–26, 35–38, 42, 67
pregnancy and vaccines, 5, 10, 58, 59, 88, 97–98, 106

recombinant vaccines, 21, 23, 89
respiratory syncytial virus (RSV), 105, 106
    vaccine for, 106
ribonucleic acid (RNA), 52–53
Roosevelt, Franklin D., 8, 35
rotavirus, 7, 24, 26, 49, 59–61, 73
    vaccine for, 17, 20
rubella, 5–7, 9, 26, 43, 97, 106
    vaccine for, 16, 26, 49–50, 67

Sabin, Albert, 38
Salk, Jonas, 35–36, 38
sexually transmitted disease, 61–63, 97, 102
smallpox, 6, 7, 9, 28–33, 43, 65–66, 68
    epidemics of, 29–31
    eradication of, 39, 43
    smallpox, 34
    vaccine for, 32–34, 66
subunit vaccines, 21–22, 102

T cells, 12–13, 14–15, 100–102, 107
thimerosal, 20, 57, 76–77
toxoid vaccines, 21
tuberculosis, 105
    vaccine for, 105

vaccination
    campaigns, 38, 43, 87
    history of, 31–33
    refusal of, 42, 65–67, 73, 80–82, 86, 88
    resistance against, 10, 41, 43, 64, 87
    schedules, 25, 26, 82, 96
Vaccine Adverse Event Reporting System
        (VAERS), 72–73
vaccines
    contamination of, 67, 77, 88
    development of, 9–10, 22, 24, 33, 35,
        37, 38, 45–53, 55–57, 59, 60, 67,
        79, 94, 96, 99–107
    ingredients in, 16, 19–20, 76, 82
    methods of delivering, 24–25
    safety of, 19, 26, 31, 36–38, 42–43,
        45–46, 48, 54–56, 59, 63–65,
        67–71, 73, 77–79, 96, 98, 104–106
    testing of, 35–38, 46–48, 57–58, 60–
        61, 87–88, 93, 101–102, 104, 107
    variolation, 29–31
variolation, 64–66, 107

Wakefield, Andrew, 74–79, 80, 86
World Health Organization, 38, 39,
        40–42, 87, 96

yellow fever, 7, 8, 10, 41
    vaccine for, 10, 24, 49, 97

Zika virus, 7, 10, 32, 97–99, 105, 106
    outbreak of, 97–98
    vaccine for, 98, 105
zoonotic viruses, 32, 53

ABOUT THE AUTHOR

Science journalist Tara Haelle has written about vaccines and other health topics for *Scientific American*, the *Washington Post*, *Wired*, and many other publications. She has discussed vaccines on National Public Radio, on TV news shows, at universities, and at immunization conferences. Her books for young readers include *Seasons, Tides, and Lunar Phases*; *Insects as Predators*; and *Insects as Parasites*.

Haelle lives in Illinois. Learn more about her work as a journalist and an educator at her website, www.tarahaelle.net. From there you can link to her health-focused parenting blog, "Red Wine and Applesauce," and to her TEDx Talk, "Why Parents Fear Vaccines."

PHOTO ACKNOWLEDGMENTS

The images in this book are used with the permission of: FDA/flickr.com (public domain), p. 5; elizabethan_victorian/Beniamino Facchinelli/Wikimedia Commons (public domain), p. 7; PACIFIC PRESS/Alamy Stock Photo, p. 9; The Science Picture Company/Alamy Stock Photo, p. 11; © Laura Westlund/Independent Picture Service, pp. 14–15, 18, 25, 100–101; © NIAID/flickr.com (CC BY 2.0), p. 23; © 2013 Gary W. Meek Photography, Inc./D/B/A PhatPixel Media/Georgia Institute of Technology, p. 24; Sarin Images/The Granger Collection, New York, p. 28; Hulton Archive/Getty Images, p. 33; © FDR Presidential Library & Museum/flickr.com (CC BY 2.0), p. 35; Photo Researchers/Science History Images/Alamy Stock Photo, p. 36; Getty Images News, p. 39; Andrew Aitchison/Corbis Historical/Getty Images, p. 40; Eric Préau/Sygma/Getty Images, p. 47; Ed Clark/The LIFE Picture Collection/Getty Images, p. 50; STR/AFP/Getty Images, p. 52; © Grand Rapids History and Special Collections, Archives, Grand Rapids Public Library, Grand Rapids, Michigan, p. 57 (Kenderick and Eldering); ton koene/Alamy Stock Photo, p. 62; Library of Congress (LC-USZC4-3147 DLC), p. 65; AP Photo/Rich Pedroncelli, p. 71; Steve Parsons/PA Images/Getty Images, p. 75; Brendan Hoffman/Getty Images Entertainment, p. 78; Sally Greenhill/Sally and Richard Greenhill/Alamy Stock Photo, p. 84; Irfan Khan/Los Angeles Times/Getty Images, p. 85; AP Photo/Amy Forliti, p. 86; Jenny Matthews/Alamy Stock Photo, p. 90; Lucas Oleniuk/Toronto Star/Getty Images, p. 95; SCHNEYDER MENDOZA/AFP/Getty Images, p. 98; KENZO TRIBOUILLARD/AFP/Getty Images, p. 104; Richard T. Nowitz/Science Source, p. 107.

Front cover and design elements: © iStockphoto.com/kolae.